"From the very beginning of the ministry I've had leading local churches, I've known the teaching of the Apostle Paul in Ephesians 4 to be catalytic for unleashing the body of Christ in full-body ministry. God did not gift apostles, prophets, evangelists, pastors (shepherds), and teachers to do all the ministry—but rather to equip the saints, the whole people of God, to do the work of ministry of building up the body of Christ. I know this is true—and so do you—but most pastors and churches have settled for ministry done by the few and observed by the many. In this book, Aaron Perry has given practical and pragmatic ways for those who dare to recover the full-body ministry of the body of Christ. It is theologically sound, engagingly written, and eminently useful."

—Jeffrey E. Greenway,
President Pro-Tempore, Allegheny West
Conference, Global Methodist Church

"Living out Paul's words 'equipping the saints to do the work of the ministry' in Ephesians 4:11–13 is a text profound in action. *Lay Leadership* is written from a pastor's heart and mind in dealing with the complexity of developing lay leadership. Dr. Perry does not shy away from the complexity of this ministry. Through personal experiences as well as wisdom from the ages the reader will find an excellent pathway to developing a flourishing lay leadership—truly living out the words of Paul. This is a much-needed book. The term 'developing lay leadership' is popular these days, yet there are very few honest resources available. I put *Lay Leadership* at the top of the list."

—Jo Anne Lyon,
General Superintendent Emerita,
The Wesleyan Church

"In a Christian world that is increasingly professionalized, Aaron gives us a much needed nudge toward organic, lay-centered ministry that is relational through and through. In winsome, easy language he leads us step by step into the kind of ministry that builds community and advances the kingdom, with real people using real gifts and responding to the very real call of God. Every church needs this teaching."

—Carolyn Moore,
lead pastor, Mosaic Church, Evans, GA

"Aaron Perry has convinced me even more that the movement of God we long for will only happen with a more complete partnership of pastors and lay people—together, the gospel impact is immeasurable! Theologically rich and practically resourceful, this book rejects the 'pastor/parishioner pyramid scheme' and equips all for ministry rooted in the church, 'wide in the world and deep in the believer.' Incredible!"

—Wayne Schmidt,
general superintendent, The Wesleyan Church

"Every pastor and congregation wants the good gifts of Jesus to run wild, wide, and deep. But how? *Lay Leadership* provides a clear and actionable plan for developing thriving lay leaders. Pastors, leaders, and congregations will benefit immediately from reading Lay Leadership."

—A. Trevor Sutton,
senior pastor, St. Luke Lutheran Church,
Lansing, MI

"Aaron Perry's seven phases for raising up and deploying lay leaders operationalizes biblical truths in an easily applied lay mobilization system. Imagine the beauty of the collective 'yes' of believers living out God's call in the world through the church. This book will help make that vision a daily reality in your congregation."

—Thomas F. Tumblin,
professor of leadership,
Asbury Theological Seminary

"*Lay Leadership* is the perfect book for the local church today. Dr. Perry does a masterful job outlining a practical and comprehensive strategy for how church leaders can effectively 'equip the saints for the work of ministry' (Ephesians 4:11–13) and care for souls in Jesus's name. This book is a much needed resource that will prove to be timeless and transcend the ever-changing eras of culture."

—Jeff Wallace,
chief strategic officer,
Student Leadership University, FL

"Central to the pastor's task is stewarding the congregation well, recognizing the people are the talents (Matthew 25:14–30). Aaron Perry is a wise and skillful guide who shares his vision and tactics for investing in lay leadership. I'm convinced that fruitful ministry in the West depends on investing in lay leaders, and this book is a wonderful place to start."

—Jesse Williams,
teaching pastor, Des Moines Gospel Chapel, WA

"For pastors who desire to see their congregations flourish and engage the work of ministry as a whole community, Aaron Perry has laid out an exceptional guide to support that vision. Theologically wise, practical, and complete, this book will give fuel to any pastor who wants to grow and support laborers for the advance of the gospel."

—Jeremy Writebol,
pastor, Woodside Bible Church Plymouth, MI;
author, *Pastor, Jesus Is Enough*

Lay Leadership

For the Care of Souls

LEXHAM MINISTRY GUIDES

Lay Leadership

For the Care of Souls

AARON PERRY

General Editor

Harold L. Senkbeil

LEXHAM PRESS

Lay Leadership: For the Care of Souls
Lexham Ministry Guides

Lexham Press, 1313 Commercial St., Bellingham, WA 98225
LexhamPress.com

Print ISBN 9781683597780
Digital ISBN 9781683597797
Library of Congress Control Number 2024934996

Series Editor: Harold L. Senkbeil
Lexham Editorial: Todd Hains, Elliot Ritzema, Abigail Stocker
Cover Design: Lydia Dahl
Typesetting: Mandi Newell
Printed in India
24 25 26 27 28 29 30 / IN / 12 11 10 9 8 7 6 5 4 3 2 1

To the many, many lay leaders I've been privileged
to lead, learn from, and serve alongside
at Calvary Community Church
and Centennial Road Church

And to my wife, Heather, whose ministry
and leadership as a lay person inspired,
tested, and refined so much of this book.

Contents

Acts 20:28

Pay careful attention to yourselves and
to all the flock, in which the Holy Spirit
has made you overseers, to care
for the church of God,
which he obtained
with his own
blood.

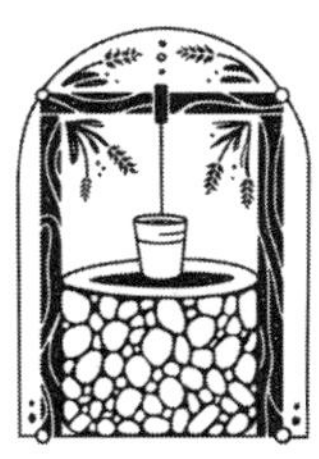

Series Preface

WHAT'S OLD IS NEW AGAIN.

The church in ages past has focused her mission through every changing era on one unchanging, Spirit-given task: the care of souls in Jesus's name. Christian clergy in every generation have devoted themselves to bringing Christ's gifts of forgiveness, life, and salvation to people by first bringing them to faith and then keeping them in the faith all life long.

These people—these blood-bought souls—are cared for just as a doctor cares for bodies. The first step is carefully observing the symptoms of distress, then diagnosing the ailment behind these symptoms. Only after careful observation and informed diagnosis can a physician of souls proceed—treating not the symptoms, but the underlying disease.

Attention and intention are essential for quality pastoral care. Pastors first attentively listen with Christ's ears and then intentionally speak with Christ's mouth. Soul care is a ministry of the Word; it is rooted in the conviction that God's word is efficacious—it does what it says (Isa 55:10–11).

This careful, care-filled pastoral work is more art than science. It's the practical wisdom of theology, rooted in focused study of God's word and informed by the example of generations past. It's an aptitude more than a skillset, developed through years of ministry experience and ongoing conversation with colleagues.

The challenges of our turbulent era are driving conscientious evangelists and pastors to return to the soul care tradition to find effective tools for contemporary ministry. (I describe this in depth in my book *The Care of Souls: Cultivating a Pastor's Heart*.) It's this collegial conversation that each author in this series engages—speaking from their own knowledge and experience. We want to learn from each other's insights to enrich the soul care tradition. How can we best address contemporary challenges with the timeless treasures of the Word of God?

In the Lexham Ministry Guides you will meet new colleagues to enlarge and enrich your unique ministry to better serve the Savior's sheep and lambs with confidence. These men and women are in touch with people in different subcultures and settings, where they are daily engaged in learning the practical wisdom of the care of souls in real-life ministry settings just like yours. They will share their own personal insights and approaches to one of the myriad aspects of contemporary ministry.

Though their methods vary, they flow from one common conviction: all pastoral work is rooted in a pastoral habitus, or disposition. What every pastor does day after day is an expression of who the pastor is as a servant of Christ and a steward of God's mysteries (1 Cor 4:1).

Although the authors may come from theological traditions different than yours, you will find a wealth of strategies and tactics for practical ministry you can apply, informed by your own confession of the faith once delivered to the saints (Jude 1:3).

Our Lord doesn't call us to success, as if the results were up to us: "Neither he who plants nor he who waters is anything, but only God who gives the growth" (1 Cor 3:7). No, our Lord asks us to be faithful laborers in the service of souls he has purchased with his own blood (Acts 20:28).

Nor does our Lord expect us to have all the answers: "I will give you a mouth and wisdom" (Luke 21:15). Jesus, the eternal Word of the Father, is the Answer who gives us words when we need them to give to our neighbors when they need them. After all, Jesus sees deeper into our hearts than we do; he knows what we need. He is the Wisdom of God in every generation (1 Cor 1:24).

But wisdom takes time. The Lord our God creates, redeems, and sanctifies merely by his words. He could give us success and answers now, but he usually doesn't. We learn over time through challenges and frustrations—even Jesus grew over time (Luke 2:52). The Lexham Ministry Guides offer practical wisdom for the church.

My prayer is that you grow in humble appreciation of the rare honor and responsibility that Christ Jesus bestowed on you in the power and presence of his Spirit: "As the Father has sent me, even so I am sending you" (John 20:21).

Father in heaven, as in every generation you send forth laborers to do your work and equip them by your word, so we pray that in this our time you will continue to send forth your Spirit by that word. Equip your servants with everything good that they may do your will, working in them that which is well pleasing in your sight. Through Jesus Christ our Lord. Amen.

Harold L. Senkbeil, General Editor
September 14, 2020
Holy Cross Day

Prayer for Lay Leadership

SINCE THE EARLIEST DAYS OF THE CHURCH, Christians have used holy Scripture to shape and inform their life of prayer. The structured prayer below invites pastors and laity to pray for the equipping, leadership, and service of all members of the church. It can be used by either individuals or groups—in which case a designated leader begins and the others speak the words in bold font.

In the name of the Father, Son, and Holy Spirit.
Amen.

O Lord, open my lips,
And my mouth will declare your praise. *Ps 51:15*

Give ear, O Shepherd of Israel, you who lead
Joseph like a flock.
**You who are enthroned upon the cherubim,
shine forth.** *Ps 80:1*

He led out his people like sheep
and guided them in the wilderness like a flock.

Ps 78:52

Surely goodness and mercy shall follow me
all the days of my life,
**and I shall dwell in the house of the
LORD forever.** *Ps 23:6*

Let us pray to the Lord.

Lord, have mercy.
Christ, have mercy.
Lord, have mercy.

That God by his word would create in us clean
hearts and renew a right spirit within us.
That he would give us eyes to see the talents
and gifts of those entrusted to our care.
That we would equip the saints for service
and build up the body of Christ.

Let us pray to the Lord.
Lord, have mercy.

That God would lead us in the paths of
righteousness for his name's sake.

That he would do great acts among us and through us.
That we would give thanks for the saints' faith in Jesus Christ and their love for his children.

Let us pray to the Lord.
Lord, have mercy.

Our Father who art in heaven
Hallowed be thy name,
Thy kingdom come,
Thy will be done on earth as it is in heaven;
Give us this day our daily bread;
And forgive us our trespasses as we forgive those who trespass against us;
And lead us not into temptation,
But deliver us from evil.
For thine is the kingdom and the power, and the glory forever and ever.
Amen. *Matt 6:9–13*

Almighty and everlasting God, by your Spirit the whole body of the church is governed and sanctified. Receive our prayers, which we offer before you for your holy church, that all members—in their vocation and ministry—may serve you in truth and godliness; through our Lord and Savior Jesus Christ. Amen.

The Lord almighty direct our days and our deeds in his peace.

Amen.

CHAPTER 1

Lead: Ministry that Runs Wild, Wide, and Deep

And the more I considered Christianity,
the more I found that while it had established
a rule and order, the chief aim of that order was
to give room for good things to run wild.
—G. K. Chesterton

THIS IS A BOOK ABOUT THE PASTORAL WORK OF leading the laity in ministry so that they become leaders as well. There's complexity and, at times, confusion to how this is done and what it entails. C. S. Lewis said that everything is complex, and if you're not content with simple answers you shouldn't complain when you encounter complex ones.[1] We shouldn't expect anything different from this topic. But when I'm imagining a leadership activity or role, it helps me to keep specific people in mind. When I think of lay leadership, I often think of Ted.

"Guys, I need you to pray for me." Coming from Ted, we took notice. He never missed our small group meeting, but asking for prayer was more than a bit out of the ordinary. We leaned in. Ted continued: "I think I need to tell my buddies I can't play basketball on Sunday mornings."

Where I would be on Sunday mornings wasn't an open question. As a pastor, my responsibilities were set. My family's responsibilities—my wife being very active in the church and my children still too young to protest—were clear. I knew where I was going to be. But for Ted, every Sunday was a choice.

For most of the year, I knew where Ted would be—in church. Ted was a committed churchman with a genuine and deep faith. But basketball season was different. The camaraderie, the fellowship, the atmosphere—these enhanced Ted's already deep love for basketball. And Ted was good at basketball. Really good. His team not only enjoyed having him; they *needed* him.

And so Ted needed prayer. Telling his team he wouldn't be playing on Sunday mornings was not a simple conversation. Ted's teammates would not understand; they would not see him the same way. Things wouldn't go back to normal quickly. But it was the choice Ted needed to make to display his faith and lead his family.

We reflected theologically on Ted's act and how it was a kind of leadership. Our group came to see Ted's action as a reflection of Christ's ministry in the world through Ted. Christ's offices not only founded my preaching in the church, but Ted's witness to the world. Yes, he could have witnessed while being present at basketball, but Ted believed his decision was not only leading as a parent in his family, but also as a part of the church and as part of the people of God. As an act of ordering his family and life, it was a *royal* act; as an act of leading worship, it was a *priestly* act; as an act of embodied witness (his teammates knew where Ted would be when he wasn't with them), it was a *prophetic* act.

On the first Sunday of basketball season, I saw Ted. So did other people in our church. And while his teammates didn't *see* him physically, they *saw* him in a fresh light. As his pastor, my calling was to help Ted fulfill his calling in the world.

Who's your Ted? Who is the person that comes to mind when you think of leading them to ministry done in the name of Jesus Christ? When faced with complexity, orient yourself by bringing this person back to mind. How does what you've read apply to *them*?

The Complexity of Ministry

It helps to keep real names and real people in mind because vocation is simple *and* complex. It is simple in that God has set some people aside for certain work within the church, but it is not always simple how the work, or ministry, of pastors and the work, or ministry, of the people interrelate. No doubt you have encountered the simplicity *and* complexity of vocation and ministry, too. At some point you have either said or been told (or both!) that ministry really is *quite simple*. True! Ministry is simple. It is service. But, also, false! Ministry is remarkably complex because ministry always involves people with rich and complicated lives. And, whether you're a pastor or a layperson who leads and serves in the church and out of faith in Christ—and I hope both pick up this book and read it, especially together!—then you understand just how complex ministry can become in the context of the local church and the pastor-layperson relationship.

Yes, ministry is both simple and complex. In a discussion on the paradox of authority in the church, G. K. Chesterton noted that "while [Christianity] had established a rule and order, the chief aim of that order was to give room for good things to run wild."[2] Consider the complexity of ministry and the complexity of the pastor-layperson relationship as ultimately a kind of paradox in service to *good*. Ministry is about good—good things done in Jesus's name and therefore by Jesus, but especially good news, the word spoken and the word made flesh through the acts of Christ's body, the church, in the world every day. The chapters that follow present specific actions that spread good in the church, by the laity of the church, and in the laity as they are transformed through service. Recall Ted's story. Good was running *wild* in the church because his influence in our group was expanding and others were seeing a man display even greater faithfulness to Christ's lordship. They were challenged to do the same. And good was running *wide* in the world because his witness was being seen by his teammates and Ted was intentional in following it up with personal witness and testimony. Finally, good was running *deep* in the believer because Ted was being formed in Christlikeness. *The work of the pastor to serve and order the church is so that good things may run wild in the church, wide in the world, and deep in the believer. And that's all about lay leadership—equipping and empowering laity for ministry in Jesus's name.* I contend that we—pastors and laity alike—cannot be faithful and ignore the opportunity that lies before us for lay leadership and ministry in the twenty-first century.

Let me clarify one of my terms. We often conceive of ministry as being *inside* the church and mission being *outside* the church. In this book, however, work in Jesus's name, whether inside or outside the church, is often lay leadership and lay ministry. Ministry in the church, whether by the pastor or the people of God, is practice for the church's mission in the world, and her mission in the world must soon offer an invitation into the mutual care of ministry that happens within the church. This isn't to say that every person in the church has equal ability or responsibility for a ministry that is "wide in the world" and "wild in the church," but to affirm that the whole church is participating in the whole church's activity as one body. Many specific actions done in Jesus's name, including singing on a praise team, holding and praying over babies in the nursery, and organizing a food drive, can serve as examples of ministry—as examples of good running wild, wide, and deep.

Conflict, Complacency, Incapacity

This is difficult work. When the pastor-lay leader relationship loses sight of its good purpose, then we create unnecessary and unhelpful tensions. There is *misguided conflict.* We forget our mission and become dull light and stale salt. This is *missional complacency.* We become discouraged at serving one another and we let opportunities to serve one another in the church slip by us. There is *ministry incapacity.*

Have you observed any of these ministry breakdowns?

1. Pastors claim and/or operate with too much authority and pastoral leadership becomes pastoral abuse; pastoral authority turns to pastoral authoritarianism.

2. Pastors act or are encouraged to act as the only ministers, and pastors get worn out from doing all or almost all of the ministry in an underactive, inactive, and underdeveloped church.
3. Pastors and laity are believed to have the very same roles, and so while the pastoral office is occupied there is little pastoral authority and decreased ministry capacity among the people. No one is setting a ministry example or leading in ministry.

Misguided conflict, missional complacency, and ministry incapacity manifest in a number of ways: little volunteering, demoralized lay leaders, a false sense of "everything being under control," a perception of few opportunities for meaningful, challenging ministry and leadership by the laity. Perhaps most discouraging of all is when this terrible trio appears as boredom with God and heavenly things.[3]

No doubt you have heard a pastor bemoan being "put on a pedestal." Perhaps it's been you. I have felt like that. The pedestal is sometimes the result of a kind of pastor-parishioner pyramid scheme. We imagine different levels of leadership in the church where the pastor has climbed the pyramid and now looks down at the rest occupying the lower levels. In this arrangement, power and authority is about ascending the pyramid. When this gets into the church's leadership imagination, then the clergy might *feel* above because the people *see* them as above. Sometimes this image gets verbalized (internally and externally) by the people like this: "*I* could never do that! *I'm* not fit for ministry!"

But it isn't only the people who believe that ministry is the work of the pastor and so function with an elevated image. Sometimes *pastors* think they are the only ones fit for ministry, too. Perhaps they wouldn't say that they are the ones fit for ministry, but their actions reveal it. Belief that pastors alone do ministry is seen in little delegation, few fresh missional endeavors, and a false sense of excellence—even perfectionism. Pastors who act like they are essential for ministry try to be everywhere and are always available.

Sometimes a pastor can feel a sense of power and indispensability by always being needed and in demand. More often, though, I believe that pastors are simply overwhelmed at even the thought of attempting a new way of addressing needs and seizing opportunities. They see a need and rush to fill it; they sense an opportunity and don't want to miss it. And then it becomes an unsustainable cycle. The need was filled and, strangely, has only gotten bigger. The opportunity was seized and now it can't be released. You can see how this might result in quite a full workload for the pastor!

How strange when the one at the top of the pyramid just keeps getting more and more tasks! Perhaps you've had a similar experience to this one of mine: I was talking to someone who said, "Pastor, I've got a great idea for a new ministry." I had been engaged in the conversation thus far, but at these words my ears really perked up. I love ministry happening in the church! I love when good things are running wild, wide, and deep! So, I was eager to hear this idea. "Tell me about it!" I replied. What followed was about ten minutes of insightful history and compelling vision. The idea was faithfully rooted in the church's past accomplishments, but the vision was properly updated to its present culture and community. The details and structure were a bit lacking, but those could be covered in time and with proper pastoral support. I was starting to sense the momentum. Then came the words that no pastor wants to hear: "And I think *you'll* do a great job running it, Pastor Aaron."

Earlier in my pastoral ministry, I would have laid out a theology of ministry until the person's eyes glazed and their mouth gaped. Underlying the comment was a belief that pastors, and only pastors, do ministry. Sometimes people don't hold to this belief tightly; sometimes that's just what they've been shown. More recently, I've learned that instead of teaching in that conversation, I need to test their commitment. Committed people can always be trained to lead and taught a stronger theology. So, we took some initial steps. We organized an interest meeting. We advertised publicly and invited personally. It was a good idea for ministry, but would it have traction or momentum? It didn't. Even the person with the idea didn't come to the meeting! Quietly, the idea died, but I was given fresh life to teach and preach that ministry is the work of all the people of God. If I had simply taken the idea and run with it, it could have continued the idea that only pastors do ministry.

So, how can we correct misguided conflicts, missional complacency, and ministry incapacity? With some theology.

Corrective Convictions

While I learned not to bring them up at every opportunity, I increasingly realized that I needed to sprinkle three key convictions throughout my leadership, teaching, and ministry.

Theological conviction #1: God the Father has only one begotten Son, Jesus Christ. A good Christology solves a lot of problems. But there's even better news: a good Christ saves the world. The devil tempted Jesus with all the kingdoms of this world. All it would cost was Jesus's worship. Peter reaffirmed this temptation when he tried to steer Jesus away from the cross (Matt 16:22). For Jesus to be King without a cross would have meant many others on their own crosses. After all, Jesus could have been a commander like so many others through human history. But his faithfulness even to the cross set him apart. And upon the faithful completion of his mission, Jesus announced that all authority—not just on earth, but in heaven—had been given to him (Matt 28:18). His authority is not limited to time and space; it is over all time and beyond all space.

What does this matter for ministry? Out of this authority, Jesus authorizes ministry! "Go!" he tells us. "Make disciples by baptizing and teaching," he commands.

What does this mean for pastoral authority? It means that all authority, including pastoral authority, flows from and is under Christ. To *have* authority means to be *under* authority. Christ is under the authority of the Father and, because of Christ's perfect obedience, the Father holds nothing back from the Son's authority. And Christ authorizes his church, including its pastors, to act. The pastor is thus not self-appointed; neither is the pastor unaccountable. The pastor is, as is all the church, under the authority of Christ, the only begotten Son. The authority of the pastor is to lead and serve in such a way that good things, like benevolence ministries, Sunday School picnics, small groups, and support systems for abused persons, may run wild under Christ's authority.

That God has only one begotten Son also means that all distinctions between pastor and laity are time-limited. The destiny of people is not to have *division*, but *fellowship* in Christ. Any complexity between pastor and laity will be removed in the fully revealed kingdom of our Lord. We might say that we look forward to a day when there is only one Pastor, the Great Shepherd, the only begotten Son.

Theological conviction #2: Ministry is the work of all the people of God. First, ministry is the work of all the people because it is the overflow of Christ's own ministry. It's not a separate ministry but Christ's continued work. Christ served the world, and the people called out from the world into Christ are to emulate their Lord in the world by, and only by, the power of his very Spirit. Ministry is a witness to the ministry of Christ![4]

Second, ministry is the work of all the people of God because ministry was given to the initial couple. The first man and woman were given royal identities—made in the image of God. The first man and woman were given priestly roles to tend and care for the garden. The first man and woman were given prophetic roles—the man to name the animals and the woman to speak the truth to the serpent (though she failed to do so).

The work of ministry dignifies the one serving and the one served. Being a *people* is a rich identity in the text of Scripture. The exodus stands out as giving the dignity and honor of being a people (Exod 19:4–7; Deut 4:20; 7:6–11). When Paul describes the people of the church as a body with great honor being given to the lesser members (1 Cor 12:21–26), this is what we should expect! God drew together the weak and dishonored to be a people, to give them honor and greatness by his presence in order not to be served, but to serve!

There is some work, some ministry, that *only* Christ can do. Only Christ, the only begotten Son, can baptize by his Spirit. And what does Christ do in baptism? Jesus the High Priest cleanses us to be priests; Jesus the enfleshed Word of God marks us out as prophets; Jesus the Christ anoints us to be royalty. As royalty, all of God's people have responsible service and leadership in the world. As prophets, all of God's people teach and train for ministry. As priests, all of God's people anoint for healing and intercede for God's people in his presence. The roles established in creation are now redeemed by the work of Christ—not in a dismissal of creation, but in its redemption.

This is quite a different approach to a theology of ministry than I often encounter in the classroom and the church. Fueled by Enlightenment language of individuality and rights, interpretations of "the priesthood of all believers" go something like this: "Why shouldn't *anyone* baptize?" "Why can't *anyone* serve communion?" Obviously, there are different theologies of ordination and different practices for the ordained in different traditions, but what the above questions miss is a theology of the laity, of the people. Missiologist Hendrik Kraemer encourages us not to start a theology of the laity with the priesthood of all believers because this can get us into conflict through its unnecessary and excessive focus on the individual.[5]

Instead, we must ground the ministry of humankind not in rights and modernity but in Christ's redemption of the created world. All human beings are priests by virtue of God's creation. We are beings who began on a mountain (Ezek 28:13–14), a point of heaven meeting earth, and were scattered to carry God's glory throughout the whole world. The only begotten Son of God truly reveals humankind's nature as the perfect mediator, the great High Priest. Humanity's priestliness is regained through Christ and in Christ. Peter picks up this metaphor and applies it to the church. The church is a royal priesthood, a holy nation (1 Pet 2:9–10).

The value of the people in ministry is captured nicely by Martin Luther. He wrote, "A cobbler, a smith, a farmer—each has the work and office of his trade, and yet they are all alike consecrated priests and bishops, and every one by means of his own work or office must benefit and serve every other, that in this way many kinds of work may be done for the bodily and spiritual welfare of the community, even as all the members of the body serve one another."[6] Ministry flows from the lives of all people who are part of the church of Jesus Christ, and their actions are ministry when they are founded on Christ. And Christ is a foundation strong enough for the whole structure built by faith! (Eph 2:19–22).

Third, ministry is the work of all the people because the people are essential to the church. It makes little sense to place so much ministry emphasis on the pastor, because while you can have a local church without a pastor, you can't have a local church without people. Hendrik Kraemer emphasizes that the free church tradition has always seen the people as an essential part of the church, not a merely accidental or simply beneficial part. A full ecclesiology requires a full affirmation of the people. There is not an active and passive part of the church. There is a rhythm of ministering and receiving ministry. There are not just leaders and followers. There is a rhythm of following and leading under the authority of Christ.

But if there is unique work for the pastor in the church, how can we describe it? How can we correct, but not overcorrect, falling into individualism and rights?

Theological conviction #3: Pastors are given so that the people of God may confess the lordship of Christ and be equipped to serve Christ (Eph 4:11–13). God the Father has only one begotten Son, Jesus of Nazareth. The first man and woman couldn't withstand temptation in a lush garden, let alone the parched desert as our Lord did. The first man and woman couldn't resist a good-looking piece of fruit, let alone all the world's kingdoms as our Lord did. Where we failed and failed and failed, Christ succeeded. And from his victory, he nourishes and cleanses us—even in the desert and from the stains of sin. When God through and by the church sets some aside for pastoral leadership and entrusts certain actions to them, it is always so that we may confess that the Great Shepherd has done for us what we could not do for ourselves.

Pastors equip the church to live out this confession in the world. But we forget our mission. We get caught up in the lusts of the flesh and the pride of life. Forbidden fruit continues to look good to eat and we are tempted to set up our mini kingdoms where we rule instead of serve. Just as the Levites were to help establish the conditions for Israel's missional faithfulness and effectiveness, so are pastors given to the church to equip the people to serve Christ. Pastors are set aside so that the church may stay focused on its collective vocation.

How easily we slip away from a ministry life, not by forgetting but by despairing. How sinister is the enemy when he convinces people that they are incapable of meaningful and faithful ministry in the name of Jesus Christ—that Christ could never have called *them*. What a gift pastoral leadership is in those times of despair to proclaim the authority that Christ has given! Leadership is never a gift given strictly to the pastor, but it often comes *through* the pastor. Authority is given so that more may be authorized. Leaders do not simply acquire followers; they raise up more leaders. The nature of this leadership—by necessity—is empowering service. Pastors cannot faithfully lead without raising up more leaders. Pastors serve by leading and lead by serving. And in so doing, they help to establish the order, the parameters, that allow good to flow over and not just fizzle out.

But it is not a one-sided relationship of one serving the other. No! What a gift the laity are to the pastor! What a beautiful service it is when the church reminds the pastor of the parameters the pastor inherits and exemplifies service and care! Just as the Israelites were God's means of caring for the Levites who had no land of their own, so the church is the means of caring for God's shepherds. I sometimes wonder where I might have wandered were it not for the church overseeing my training and ordination.

Ministry Foundations

Remember the image of the pyramid? Let's reframe it. Rather than moving *up* the pyramid or being raised above the people, pastoral leadership is establishing firm footing for the people to take their own steps in service to Christ. Just as parents provide strong foundations for their children to take secure steps, pastors are there to support ministry—and even provide a little nudge in that direction. Can you picture a pastor who played that role? In my life, I think of Pastor Daryl and Pastor John: two men who coached, encouraged, prayed, cheered on, and cheered up along the way as I was learning about Christ and how he was acting in and through my life.

Rather than moving up the pyramid, leaders move to the foundation in support. As mentioned above, the foundation and impetus and energy of ministry is Christ and his Spirit. Christ is "behind" and "beneath" it all. Christ, by his Spirit, is in it all. Christ is the foundation and model of ministry. And Christ's ministry was directed to the Father. So, Christ provides a model and sets the direction in ministry. We aim to serve God by serving in the world and we serve in the world by aiming at the Father. The power, the source of strength for this ministry, is also God: God the Holy Spirit, given through the accomplished work of Christ, empowers the whole church for ministry.

Roman Catholic Bishop Robert Barron affirms that all are called to ministry in the name of Jesus Christ just as all are called to holiness. While only some are called to poverty, all are called to detachment from the goods of the world so that the world may seek attachment to God.[7] And while only some are called to celibacy, all are called to chastity because faithfulness within marriage is a sign of Christ's faithfulness to his church. Any action, primacy, activity, and giving of the pastor is either a reminder of what Christ alone can do and has done *or* a model to be repeated in its own way by the laity in the world.

Leaders do not ascend the pyramid to receive the support of the lower levels. No, leadership in the church is to support ministry that flows from Christ and aims at serving the Father.

Recognizing the Challenges

Of course, this conception is not without practical challenges. There will always be a tendency to understand the people, the laity, as inactive, secondary, less important, passive, receptive in the life of the church. The accuser, Satan, has consistently done this degrading and demeaning work, tempting the woman by suggesting she was less than she truly was or by convincing us that humble origins mean ongoing humiliation. God gives pastors to remind the people of the dignity of human nature and the unique accomplishments of Christ.

As a pastor, I faced the strange irony of people who simultaneously believed they didn't have the capacity for ministry or service but did believe they had the authority to call the pastor to accomplish their ministry ideas. I've also encountered pastoral colleagues who simply forgot or didn't account for the fact that their people spend just a fraction of the time in the church that the pastor does. A missional mindset can slip from the layperson's mind, perhaps, even more easily. Just a little bit of ministry math proves the point. The full-time pastor who works around fifty hours a week and receives four weeks of vacation each year spends approximately 2,400 hours in vocational, ministry-related activity every year. It would take the highly committed volunteer who spends two hours a week in ministry activities (not including corporate worship) *over twenty years* to put in the same amount of time.

It's no wonder, then, that it is always a challenge to raise up more leaders. Leadership—especially pastoral leadership—means not degrading followers but building them up. If we leave this leadership to the laity—to lead themselves, to advocate for themselves—then they will see too significant a distinction between people and pastor, and we are already off on the wrong foot.

The pastor is to free the laity for ministry by training, resourcing, equipping. So when we describe lay leadership, we must not diminish it as though it is a second-class kind of leadership, the junior varsity kind of leadership. Lay leadership does not mean a lower kind of leadership; it doesn't mean lower expectations; it doesn't mean unqualified. *It is simply—profoundly—leadership by the people of God as service to God in the church and the world in a grand variety of ways.* And resources, like pastors, are supplied so that the people may do this work faithfully and effectively. The Father has drawn a people together through his Son, the Lord Jesus, equipped them with undershepherds of the Great Shepherd (1 Pet 5:1–4), and empowered them by his Spirit for ministry in the world.

Naming the Opportunities

What great capacity the people of God have for ministry, for good work in the church and world, by the ministry of Christ and the power of the Spirit! Ministry is faith and love made visible; the love of God made visible by the power of the Spirit through the ministry of the people of God. And the opportunity is ripe for lay leadership and ministry. The time is right for God's love to be made visible through the ministry of his people in the world.

Lay leadership and ministry challenges three misguided metanarratives that Christians encounter in the world, which Charles Farhadian names as the Enlightenment, Marxism, and postmodernity.[8] First, because lay ministry is built on the foundation of Christ, it challenges the Enlightenment narrative that the story that gives energy and logic to one's life is bound up in the mechanisms of the world. The world needs to see a different story and encounter a different Lord. Second, because lay ministry is the ongoing work of the Lord who offered his life in love and faithful service to God, it runs counter to the idea that social progress comes only through conflict and war. Salvation came not by inflicting violence, but by suffering it faithfully. Finally, because lay ministry bears witness to being under the yoke of a Lord who demands nothing less than complete allegiance and an entire life, it runs counter to the postmodern belief in the unlimited individual whose opportunity/responsibility it is to chisel out any identity they may wish.

Being the church is a wonderful adventure of serving the unchanging Christ in an ever-changing world, consistently translating our words and reorienting our work both for greater faithfulness to our Lord and greater effectiveness in his world until we are caught up in the unchanging community of the Triune God. How important is this stability of life and identity in an otherwise fluctuating world!

Last century, arguably the most famous and influential Christian in the English-speaking world was a layman. C. S. Lewis influenced countless people by using the technology of his day: radio and the printing press. His imagination and logic drew many into thoughtful dialogue and abiding faith. The time is ripe for the laity, the people of God, to step into new technologies as well. It would be a grave error to focus too much attention on the technologies and less on the content, but the world is at the fingertips of every person.

Karl Barth noted the increasing means of teaching and spreading the gospel via technological growth.[9] Technical opportunities for bearing witness, of course, required more training and skill development. New technologies also provide opportunities for new gifts to be discerned or the form of old gifts to be freshly conceived. But, Barth warned, pastors must pay attention to the tempo that comes alongside technological advancements and their deployment. In the midst of new opportunities and technological advancements, Barth emphasized rest. Rest is in God and rest is from God.[10] Rest, rather than an unceasing pace, allows appropriate scrutiny of the message being proclaimed and the content being generated. Perhaps another reason why the laity need to be empowered in ministry is to help the pastor to rest appropriately in God.

In this screen-driven culture, it can become even more expected that pastors—because they are so often on screen—are the real and only teachers and ministers. The opportunity here is that the laity are *not* on the screen. What a reminder to us all that Christ's kingship was both hidden and established on the cross. Christ's kingship was hidden from all but those with eyes of faith, yet this seeming erasure from the world was his being lifted up. The laity have an opportunity to avoid a media-driven role and set of expectations to lead in a hidden way, thereby bearing witness to Christ and the witness of Christ.

Good Running Wild, Wide, and Deep

I hope that the idea of good things running wild in the church (classes, discipleship conversations), wide in the world (evangelism, works of mercy), and deep in the believer (sanctification and Christlikeness) is ringing in your ears and sinking into your heart. *The work of the pastor to serve and order the church is so that good things may run wild in the church, wide in the world, and deep in the believer. And that's all about lay leadership.*

Pastors raise up lay leaders so that good can run wild in the church. Terry walked into my office a troubled man. He observed a lot of suffering and a lot of opportunity. He spoke up, and I can still hear his Nova Scotian accent: "Pastor Aaron, they're a forgotten generation." Terry was a volunteer chaplain in the hospital and a frequent volunteer in our region's nursing homes. Hardly a Sunday passed that he wasn't leading a service, and never did a week pass that he wasn't the presence of Christ in some lonely places.

Terry was troubled because he saw so many elderly people who were forgotten. Some of them had been committed church people before they were put into care facilities. Some of them had never been to church before. Both needed to be remembered. All Terry needed was a bit of permission for good to run wild. Under Terry's leadership, we developed a team of people who were in nursing homes and the homes of shut-ins every week.

And then Liz caught the vision. We started taking flowers on a regular basis to brighten rooms.

I didn't do a whole lot so that Terry and Liz could thrive. But I was part of a chain of pastors who had proclaimed Christ and equipped them up to see that their ministry mattered. Good was running wild in the church.

Pastors raise up lay leaders so that good can run wide in the world. Ministry goes wide in the world because Christ's lordship knows no geographic bounds. The reign of Christ is never strictly local and so the ministry of Christ is carried wide. Christians are on the move and carry the good news of Christ with them and communicate the good news of Christ in ministry. Ministry is about good things going wide in the world because Jesus Christ is the center and edge of a movement.

Just as the pastor understands ministry in the church because of the hours spent in that context, so often the people know what ministry in the world should look like. The pastor must be intent not only in knowing what it looks like to be living and working in the world, but to give platform and space for the people of God to be teachers. The "missionaries" should be allowed to teach the church.

Pastors raise up lay leaders so that good can run deep in the believer. Ministry is about the good news going *deep* in the believer. Bishop Robert Barron says it like this: "Keep in mind that Jesus himself, in person, is the seed sown. ... In you, let the seed be down deep, where it can't be stolen, scorched, or choked."[11] But we don't do this ministry on our own. Ministry is not a gift we craft and curate, wrap up and set before our Lord. Ministry is a response to the gospel, and it is the ongoing work of Christ who took on the nature of a servant.

Because ministry is Christ at work in us, aimed at the Father and empowered by the Holy Spirit, ministry is sanctifying. Actions that, in faith, witness to the reign and rule of Christ are not only prompted by the Holy Spirit but used by the Holy Spirit to make the believer like Christ. For John Wesley, this ministry included feeding the hungry, clothing the naked, hosting and helping strangers, visiting the sick, teaching the uneducated, and challenging the wrongdoer and edifying the just. For me, whenever I crouch down on my knees to play with two-year-olds in their classroom on a Sunday, I don't rise the same person. In this ministry, by the Spirit, *good* is running deep.

Conclusion

The connection of deep, wild, and wide is unbreakable. They are all needed. Just like the creation as a whole is very good, so do the contexts of good belong together. When ministry is wild and deep, then there is a lively church and transformed believers, but if it is not wide then it has no global mission. When ministry is wild and wide but not deep, there is no transformed believer. And when ministry is deep and wide but not running wild in the church, there is no local church displaying the lordship of Christ in life.

Pastors, you care for souls so that God's people may live out fullness in Christ. It is only Christ who does this work, so remember that your soul, too, is cared for by the Great Shepherd, the High Priest (1 Pet 5:1–4). You, too, are part of the people, God's royal priesthood (1 Pet 2:9). But as you lead, may you intercede like Moses, who asked to be wiped out if God did not work through the people of Israel (Exod 32:31–35). May the burden of your people rest on your heart even as it is consistently given over to the one greater than Moses (Heb 3:1–6). The pastor who intercedes in that way for the local church is emulating not only the Great

Lawgiver but the High Priest who was offered up as a sacrifice in place of his people. Why do you lead like this? Because it is how our Lord continues to work through his people in the world. The laity, the people of God, will lead priestly lives, sacrificial lives of ministry, by virtue of the Great High Priest.

CHAPTER 2

Cast: Helping Others to See What You See

For what you see and hear depends a good deal on where you are standing: it also depends on what sort of person you are.

—C. S. Lewis

PASTORS LEAD THE PEOPLE OF GOD SO THAT good things run wild in the church, wide in the world, and deep in the believer. But leadership is a complex phenomenon. It has been variously conceived as certain behaviors, necessary skills, a relationship, and a unique blend of all of these put into processes and systems. Not only is leadership complex; it is also mysterious. Leadership has also been conceived as an ability—perhaps an ability that only great men and great women have.

If pastors lead in such a way that good runs wild, wide, and deep, what does this leadership include? Is it behaviors, skills, a sheer ability? There are six key components to leading the people of God in a way that cares for the soul and facilitates wide, wild, and deep ministry: casting vision, asking for commitment, designing tasks, training for effective service, tracking effectiveness, and expressing thanks. Each of these components is the subject of a chapter in this book.

Growing up the youngest of three boys had its disadvantages. (My brothers will gladly tell you all the advantages.) Being the smallest and least educated of us at any point meant that I was not much of a match for them in wrestling or wits. I was so uncompetitive in one particular game, *Trivial Pursuit*, that my older brothers only competed against each other. One of the game's distinguishing features is its iconic game-scoring pie with its wedges of various colors, each representing a different field of knowledge. Players compete to fill the pie with wedges by answering questions from pop culture, arts and entertainment, sports, history, and so on. To win the game, you needed to show your knowledge across various domains. Imagine that scoring pie and those little wedges representing the various practices of leadership that go into leading the laity in ministry, especially so that it is pastoral leadership that cares for the soul. Just like *Trivial Pursuit* required a full array of different-colored wedges, so does leadership require a variety of competencies.

However, just as in a game of *Trivial Pursuit*, the wedges don't need to be filled in a particular order. I will flesh them out in a logical order, but rarely does organizational life, including the rhythm of church, perfectly follow logic. Life develops according to its own logic. There's a rationale, but it's sometimes hidden. As a way of expressing my frustration at not being included in this game, I would sometimes jam the wedges into the scoring pies upside down and sideways. It's what little brothers do. While the wedges that fill in the pie of the diagram have a certain flow in this book, it might be that the Spirit prompts you to focus on one or another in a different order. My only encouragement is not to force the "wedges" just so that they fit. Leadership is not simply an order to impose; it's a dance to be enjoyed. Leading laity for the care of souls will take the state of the flock into consideration as these responsibilities are implemented and developed under the Spirit's direction.

Seeing Is Being and Leading

"The first responsibility of a leader is to define reality," said Max DePree.[12] I used to disagree with him. When I first heard the phrase, I bristled. "Define reality? Who gets to define reality but God?"

Of course, that's true. God alone defines reality. Better, God Defines Reality. And all the capitals mean something. God's own Reality is different from how you and I are real. God is not just one being among several; God is other than our reality. God is the context of our reality. To use Paul Tillich's phrase, God is the ground of being. By contrast, our reality is not just something *out there.* I, too, am part of reality. And so are you. We can't help but define it. God's Defining gives it a context; our defining recognizes it, names it, puts words to what we see—including ourselves and other people.

If "defining reality" seems a bit strange, you could think of the first responsibility of leadership as *seeing.* To define reality is to see it truly. And that's what leaders need to be able to do.

Now, this act of leadership—defining reality or seeing truly—can be done arrogantly or humbly, foolishly or wisely, poorly or well. Arrogant and foolish reality defining, arrogant and foolish seeing, forgets that one is part of reality. This leader acts as though they are outside reality and can see the whole, pretending that reality is under the control of their words. Augustine was adamant that such arrogance could not see truly. In his search for God, not yet submitted to God, Augustine realized that pride had puffed up his face, swelling his eyes shut.[13] Pride blinds us!

By contrast, humble and wise leadership seeks God's wisdom in defining reality and seeing truly. In the biblical narrative, it is God whose words bring creation to being; it is God and God alone who sees without limit. God doesn't just see the outward, but also the heart (1 Sam 16:7); his eyes are everywhere, always keeping watch of good and evil (Prov 15:3). God's eyes range over the earth, finding faith and folly (2 Chr 16:9).

But God does not simply see. God gives sight! In one of his most memorable teachings on leadership (Mark 10:42–45), Jesus brought the Twelve together and told them not to lord their authority over one another. Instead, greatness means serving, and he's the example! He, the Son of Man, came to serve. But dig a bit deeper. What had prompted this little aside was a brotherly duo setting themselves apart from the other ten. James and John had pulled Jesus aside, seeking his favor.

"What do you want me to do for you?" Jesus had asked (Mark 10:36). And what did they want? Prominence. Greatness. Positions of honor. Their misguided notion of leadership had prompted Jesus's lesson. But they weren't the only ones who needed it. The other ten had become indignant (Mark 10:41). They were after greatness, too.

Then Mark's Gospel draws a profound contrast. As he is leaving Jericho, Jesus encounters a blind man who is also seeking Jesus's favor. Notice what Jesus asks him; it's the very same question he posed to James and John. "What do you want me to do for you?" (Mark 10:51). The blind man doesn't want greatness. *He wants to see.* Jesus restores his sight, and a new follower joins the entourage.[14]

What a story of leadership! What a story of defining reality and seeing! Defining reality, seeing reality truly, is the first job of leadership because it can only be done when the would-be leader is humble enough to seek the One who gives sight. Humble leaders recognize that without God, they are simply blind guides leading blind followers, which Jesus also spoke about in Matthew 15. This humble seeing recognizes that there is a reality outside the self that can be seen—praise God!—but that is outside the seer's control and command. No wonder C. S. Lewis said, "For what you see and hear depends a good deal on where you are standing: it also depends on what sort of person you are."[15]

See Something? Say Something!

There is nothing worse than a leader who doesn't see reality. When a leader can rally others to action but can't see reality truly, they are a dangerous leader. Pastors who do not know God and do not seek God are a danger to many souls. They are not seeing and should not be leading. But almost as bad as the blind leader is the seeing leader who stays silent.

If you see something, say something. Have you seen those security signs in an airport or shopping mall? The idea is that security is everyone's responsibility. The sign encourages everyone to look around and to speak up if something seems suspicious. But seeing makes no leadership difference if what is seen is not communicated. Pastors are to see something and to say something.

Now, leadership is not only looking for what's wrong; it is also looking for what's right, what's possible, what's coming. Casting is about determining reality, which includes a better future that points to the kingdom of God and the reign of Christ. Pastors see reality in Christ and speak that reality through Christ.

Casting Problems and Casting Power

Even if you agree that leadership is casting, you can be tempted to do triple takes and to get tongue tied. Many of us have either been, followed, or seen the effects of a leader who defined reality arrogantly, who thought they always saw clearly and then spoke immediately. And we certainly don't want to repeat that leadership!

Pastors are also wary of increasing cultural skepticism toward spiritual leadership. The rise of smooth-talking preachers has not been helpful to conscientious leaders, especially pastors who are sensitive to power dynamics. It is relatively easy to worry that others might see something just because the pastor said something.

Seeing also takes a lot of effort. It's hard work to know the conditions of the flock and the world! Just as a lot of our brain's energy is devoted to physical seeing, so a lot of our spiritual energy is devoted to seeing.

Finally, when you're intent on seeing some things, you will miss seeing others. If you're driving down a road, focused on seeing the road ahead, you can't see the rest of your surroundings at the same time. Much of your peripheral sight is a blur so that the road and other vehicles can be seen clearly.

But here's some good news. God is not only the *source of sight*; God is also the *means of seeing*. C. S. Lewis wrote, "I believe in Christianity as I believe that the Sun has risen, not only because I see it, but because by it I see everything else."[16] Psalm 36:9 says, "in your light we see light." Jesus Christ, the Son, gives us sight and the Holy Spirit enables us to see. And both the Son and the Spirit enable us to speak! The Word of God, the Son of God, is the source of words, and the Breath of God, the Spirit of God, carries our words from our mouths. First John 1:3 combines sight and speech and fellowship: "We proclaim to you what we have seen and heard, so that you also may have fellowship with us. And our fellowship is with the Father and with his Son, Jesus Christ." All Christian leadership—whether by the pastor or the laity—is an act of devotion and faith in this God.

Casting Metaphors

Up to now, I have avoided a word that so often goes with "casting," and that is the word "vision." Of course, I've been talking about vision because to see is to have vision, but too often "vision casting" is too narrowly understood. People are familiar with the notion that leaders are visionaries, which is true. But some otherwise exceptional leaders exhibit less influence than they might because they don't think they are visionaries. Not every leader will consider "vision casting" as one of their strengths. But while it's true that leaders—both pastors and lay leaders—must cast vision, there are various forms of casting vision.

Vision casting is like casting a story on the screen. Probably the most common way to think of casting a vision is to create a picture or a little movie in another's imagination. And this is a fine metaphor. Casting a vision is like projecting a movie on a screen. In this way, to cast means to tell a story, to present a picture of reality so that others can see it. It needs to be on display. Leadership is seeing, and what you see needs to be seen by others as well. Casting means seeing a story unfold in a faithful and fruitful way. Grow in casting by developing vivid language, practicing the telling of stories, widening your vocabulary. Try to develop illustrations and pictures drawn from a variety of interests and vocations in the world.

Vision casting is like casting actors in a play. To cast in a play means to put the right actor in the proper role. And when the actor fits the role, we see how they were "born to play the part." Likewise, the pastor "casts" by seeing the roles of church members, as well. The pastor is neither the director nor the producer of the play, but the pastor can serve as a casting agent by consistently reminding the actor of the role in which she's already been cast. Ministry is the part that the church plays—even if it feels that God has picked the wrong people for the role. God has already selected the actor and given the role; the pastor just reminds the actor.

Hendrick Kraemer, a twentieth-century Dutch missiologist and theologian, reminds us that the church is the people of God.[17] There is an identity that comes with being a people. The church is not a work force, capable of bringing about the pastor's vision. No! The pastor sees the church not as a work force or a task force but as a unique and personal body—*the* body of Christ in this world, and *the* body of Christ animated by the Spirit of God. And the pastor must say this is who the church is.

Casting vision in this way might become quite personal. The pastor might see a role for one of the people in the church to take on. They see a chance for good to run deep in the believer if they take on a certain responsibility. And it is always helpful to remind people of how individual ministries fit into the overall life of the church in worship, fellowship, discipleship, and mission.

Vision casting is like casting off pseudo-identities. "I'll always just be a ______." I cannot tell how many times I heard a variation of that phrase on ministerial development committees. Given to help people develop and discern a call to ministry, our committee would encounter initially confident young people whose negative, internal self-talk would eventually get vocalized. They were captive to a false identity not rooted in Christ. As a pastor, I also encountered pseudo-identities of God's holy and dearly loved people who saw themselves as the daughters of divorce, the sons of alcoholics, the victim of adultery, the addict, the bankrupt.

Oh, how quickly the people of God can take the bonds of the enemy! How quickly the people of God can see themselves as illegitimate children! Within this self-diminishing motif, the enemy of our souls has two great tactics: to make people think less of themselves and then to tempt them to become bitter at this self-critique. How nasty and vicious we can be as personal critics *and* then be bitter at how unfair we are as critics! The pastor sees the identity of each Christian and of the church in Christ. And the pastor casts vision by casting off those false identities. How beautiful it is to sit before someone and tell them they are not the son of a drunk or the daughter of an adulterer, but a beloved child of God! The people of God, the laity, are led when the pastor casts off these curses and casts the children of God in their role as ministers. And how beautiful when the people of God affirm that others, too, are not who they've been told they are, but that they belong to God.

Vision casting is like casting seed. When my house was built, no one cared about the lawn. Developers came in, scraped off the topsoil, put down a concrete slab, and built a house. Then they put sod on the front lawn. The backyard? Well, that was my problem. Now, the previous owner was rather successful at removing rocks, spreading earth, and planting seed—except for one little patch of mud that wouldn't grow grass. So, I bought earth and I cast some seed on it and I put some more earth on it. Then I watered it. You couldn't see the seed I had cast, but it was there—dying, growing, budding. I could just see the grass poking through. But my boys couldn't, and they tilled that little patch of lawn as though it was going to be a mini garden. I was back to casting, again. I bought seed, cast it on the lawn, and threw down some soil to dress it. You couldn't see the seed I had cast, but it was there—dying, growing, budding. I could just see the grass poking through. But my boys couldn't. And, once again, they tilled that little patch of lawn as though it was going to be a mini garden. I won't tell you how many times this happened, but eventually, grass grew. And then everyone could see it.

The leader's work of casting vision is sometimes similar. You cast little stories of potential growth and opportunity and ministry, and they go unseen. They are buried, covered over. And perhaps they get trampled on or watered down by people who can't see them. But you cast the seed again. And it grows. And eventually that vision is seen. And take heart! God sees the growing seed even if we can't (Mark 4:26–27).

Vision casting is like casting a fishing line. I don't fish. I doubt I'll ever be a fisherman, but I am amazed at their patience, skill, and determination. I have a friend who can tell me all about fly fishing and the various kinds of bait used to catch fish. The leader's work of casting vision can take a similar approach. Perhaps you don't see yourself casting a vision on a screen, but you're good at making personal connections with many individuals. Your casting work is like selecting the right bait to catch that fish. Now, I don't mean this in a manipulative kind of way, even though it can take that turn. I mean, your ability for personal connection allows you to present a picture that is uniquely meaningful to individual people. You see in them and in their future what they can't see, but once you present it to them, they are drawn to it because the vision is a fit.

Vision casting is like fitting a cast. When I was thirty years old, I cut my pinky finger down to the bone. The skin, nerve, tendon, artery—every bit of it was sliced through. It required a fairly extensive surgery to repair the damage. I still have the scars, but it gives me a nice excuse for my suffering golf game. During recovery, I was fit with a synthetic cast that would immobilize my hand to allow for healing but that was also removable for rehabilitation purposes. It worked perfectly. I regained a great deal of mobility in my finger while protecting the very tender and compromised tendon as it healed.

Sometimes casting vision is providing kinds of casts that allow for healing. There is controlled ministry, controlled opportunities for service, but then also appropriate support for recovery and healing.

Casting Opportunities

Just as there are various metaphors for casting vision, so are there various opportunities to do so. Vision casting can happen slowly, over structured time. It can also happen quickly, in a moment. It can happen one-on-one, and it can happen in a group or before a crowd. Think about how the caring work of vision casting can happen in these four ways.

Soak. Pastors lead souls in ministry by taking time to unfold a theology of identity in Christ and a theology of ministry. The vision casting should go into the details and corners of doctrine and life.

This can be a book study, a Bible study, a sermon series, a small group study, a series of social media videos. Allow people to be with the material for a period of time over weeks and even months. If you are doing vision casting on Sunday mornings, then consider pairing it with material that reiterates the teaching through home studies and via social media. Remember that doctrine, right teaching, provides a vision of reality.

Splash. Even when your teaching content is not explicitly casting the vision and identity of ministry, splash your vision casting into sermons, worship time, and ministry highlights. Consider having a monthly moment that highlights a ministry in the church. Tell the stories of laypeople who are leading in ministries in the church and the stories of laypeople making a difference by how they minister through their work. The opportunities for video-based stories are increasing. Make sure that the importance of the ministry and lay minister is underscored by the quality of the storytelling. Make sure the beauty and brilliance of Christ that you see shining through the ministry and minister is as easily seen by all others, too, by the quality of video, audio, or communication you're using.

Sprinkle. Not every story can be told as a saga or with the above commitment it takes to soak and splash. So, sprinkle stories of ministry into your sermons and into personal conversation. Share how you've seen the people of God at work in the church and world. A simple graphic or photo combined with a well-crafted Facebook or Instagram post can encourage many spirits without rearranging your schedule or requiring significant production.

Spritz. Caring parents everywhere carry little spray bottles to refresh their children at theme parks, amusement parks, and local parks. How refreshing is a little spritz of water when the sun is beating down! As you become a leader who notices ministries, you will naturally cast vision by spritzing those in ministry with encouraging words. Ken Blanchard calls this "catching people doing something right."[18] As you see something being done right, say something. Leaders are refreshers!

Conclusion

Vision casting as part of leading the people of God for the care of souls must be grounded in reality—the reality of the resurrected Christ. It is not wishful thinking. This reality is simultaneously beyond our imagination and rooted in the real world. It requires a kind of resurrection plausibility. As we cast vision, it is the reality of the risen Christ revealed in the believer, the church, and the wider world that we are describing.

If you are a natural skeptic, you will need to keep that tendency on the shelf. Pastoral leadership means leading in faith, too. And, depending on the context, you will need to help others to stow their skepticism for the time being, too. One way that skepticism shows up is by asking "how?" over and over again. Andy Stanley calls this "how-ing an idea to death."[19]

While you give freedom to avoid the death strokes of "how," you can simultaneously give space for the laity to provide their own know-how. The people of God are often wonderfully skilled at refining, expanding, and even chastening vision. Likewise, the pastor might be the one who clarifies and sharpens a vision that bubbles up among the people. Karl Barth pointed out that the laity, the people, make fruitful preaching by asking ongoing questions of the preaching and offering reflective answers to the preaching.[20] This ongoing conversation centered on the word of God can be a great place of vision casting, refining, and expanding. Pastor and laity should consider having both formal and informal conversations around the proclaimed word with vision casting in mind.

Finally, always be casting. In conversation, in sermons, in staff meetings, help others to see what you see. People forget the mission. People forget their identity in Christ. People forget the importance of the life of the church against the busyness of their own lives. Remind the people and allow yourself to be reminded of the saving work of God in Jesus Christ and of the future that is being pursued in Christ, of the future that Christ is bringing to and through his people.

CHAPTER 3

Ask: Inviting Others into the Work of God

You do not have because you do not ask.
—James 4:2 NRSV

"PASTOR RON, YOU'RE REALLY WEIRD."

"Huh?"

"That's what I would say to you if you were an insurance salesman and you never asked me to buy life insurance."

Pastor Ron had been visiting a peripheral church attender for a few weeks. They had built a rapport. They had talked about the superficial and the serious. Pastor Ron had been "calling on" Peripheral Pete, but finally Peripheral Pete called out Pastor Ron. "If you sold insurance and never asked me to buy it, I'd think you were really weird."

Pastor Ron had done everything he thought a pastor was supposed to do. He had visited, cared, prayed, listened. *But he never made an ask.* Any ask. And Peripheral Pete saw the tension. People who sell insurance eventually ask you to buy it. Why wasn't this pastor asking for anything?

Christian organizations can be known for having great vision but poor implementation. The first job of the leader is to define reality—to see something and to say something. And right after that, it's to *ask someone*. Implementation can't happen without a request for help. My friend Kelly, who is in sales, once remarked that "inspirational vision-dumpers" might think it's obvious that people will just know what to do in response to the vision. Here was Kelly's reality check to me: "It isn't. Ask."

Why Don't We Ask?

Assuming people already know what to do and that they already feel invited to join are just two reasons why pastors and leaders don't make the ask. Pastor Ron certainly isn't alone. So, why don't pastors and leaders ask for others to sign up, join in, hop on, and take responsibility so that good things can run wild, wide, and deep?

People don't ask because they consider any asking as asking too much. People are seen as too busy and we don't want to make them busier. We see people with families and jobs and hobbies. Pastors also have families and jobs and hobbies. Surely the other person with such a full life can't—maybe, we dare to know, *shouldn't*—take on more responsibility. But jobs, families, and hobbies shouldn't preclude participation in the church and in mission. Is the pastor's family called to ministry together? Of course! Family, too, is under the lordship of Christ. Is the pastor's family the only family called to minister together? Of course not! My friend Curtis has extensive experience in retail management and in the pastorate. He put it like this to me: "I have heard it often: 'Don't ask too much.' But I have found that people will rise to the occasion and will exceed expectations when the expectations are clear."

There's a sinister edge to this reluctance. Sometimes we have asked, and we have given clear expectations, but they were too little. Here's what Curtis went on to tell me: "Ask too little and you get just that." Sometimes we dare to ask but only ask for little—and people deliver! In fact, sometimes they deliver even less than what was requested because the initial request was so small. Sometimes a small request feels insignificant. Notice the double-edge of this sword: the pastor, hesitant to ask, makes a small request; the parishioner, willing to say yes, thinks their contribution is insignificant. There's disappointment all the way around. Now the pastor is both more reluctant to ask and the person is less likely to say yes. The Pareto Principle—the 80/20 rule, that 20 percent of the people are doing 80 percent of the work—often applies to the church. Frankly, the church can have a complacency problem.

Another reason that people don't ask is because asking can feel manipulative.[21] We have all known someone who could ask anyone for anything, and get it. Even if the request wasn't sinister, the other's interests weren't completely taken into consideration, and I would guess that at some point this ability didn't have a good outcome. While the pastor or leader who pauses to ask about the ethics of asking is exhibiting a good instinct, this ethical analysis can also cause asking paralysis.

Third, people don't ask because they can feel guilty about not doing what they are asking someone else to do. This, in my experience, is doubly true of pastors—especially pastors who are often working solo. If the pastor or leader hasn't been trained in leadership, then they might think that asking is about getting rid of tasks and duties they don't want to do. The reluctant asker has in mind a picture of worker-bees doing menial or mundane tasks. Because of the mysterious nature of a pastor's work, this might even feel threatening to the pastor. If the pastor is seeking help with certain duties that they could perform, then it might be even more unclear to the church what the pastor is doing.

Finally, people don't ask because rejection hurts! Nobody wants to be told no. It is easy and commonplace to feel personally bound up in every ask and to feel personally punted in every rejection.

Pastors and leaders: We must get over our fear of asking. I say this as much to myself as to anyone else. Asking is scary, difficult, challenging. (If it isn't, then I envy you, but I also encourage you to ensure you have accountability. If you don't think twice about making requests, then you might not think twice about other ways of treating people, either.) Here's why dealing with our fear is so important: We don't get over our fear of asking just to be over our fear of asking. We don't get over this fear because it will make our professional lives easier. On the contrary! When we ask more people, more widely, and for bigger commitments, then leadership will certainly get tougher and more challenging. So, why get over this fear? So that good things can run wild in the church, wide in the world, and deep in the believer. Henri Nouwen puts it brilliantly: "Are we willing to be converted from our fear of asking, our anxiety about being rejected or feeling humiliated, our depression when someone says, 'No, I'm not going to get involved in your project'? When we have gained the freedom to ask without fear, to love [asking] as a form of ministry, then [asking] will be good for our spiritual life."[22] Asking to join in, step up, and take responsibility in the work of God is good for the spiritual life—of the asker and the asked.

Christ Calls Before the Pastor Asks

My friend Dr. John Drury says it like this: "Christ calls those whom he wants to himself... and he wants them all!"[23] Scripture testifies to two callings. There is, first, a calling to God, a calling to be with Christ. And there is, second, a calling (or several) to a task, a role, a duty, a job, a work.

Ken Carder and Laceye Warner write, "God is creative: sending anyone to go anywhere, to do anything ... despite the risks, disrepute, obstacles."[24] When the pastor or leader is asking someone to join up with some ministry or missional task—some way of fulfilling the second call—it must always be kept in mind that it is not the first kind of call. The call of Christ to himself comes first. The ask is always secondary.

Christ's call to himself is specific. He does not call us to another Savior; we are called to know him and to be with him. But his call to serve in the church and to go into the world often requires further discernment. We ask so that people can discern the specifics of their calling. And if this specific opportunity isn't right, then the answer should be "No." Every "Yes" is a "No" to something else, and every "No" is potentially a "Yes" to something else. Pastors and leaders ask so that the church has a chance to discern God's call rightly and truly and specifically.

Asking to join in meaningful mission and ministry is an opportunity for the asked to set aside pointless toil. Will Willimon writes, "We yield to the adventure of a life free of the ideology of personal autonomy that so enslaves this [Western] culture. We are owned, commandeered for God, yoked to a manner of service wherein is perfect freedom."[25] This isn't just true of the ordained! No! To pretend or to act as though the pastor is the only one under the yoke of Christ is to limit Christ's lordship. Christ is Lord and Master not just of the pastor, and not just of the church, but of the whole world. When pastors and leaders ask, we give opportunity for people to express that lordship in specific ways. It's an invitation to specific service, wherein is perfect freedom. We ask people to step up and join in ministry and service and leadership not because we believe in the self and self-fulfillment, but because we believe in God. We ask people to join in leadership because it's Christ we're following together.

Leadership Dispositions and Holy Ask-Attitudes

Leadership is about disposition, one's natural way of approaching the world. When it comes to asking others to join in, sign up, and get involved, I like to think of disposition as an "ask-attitude." And if asking is a ministry and is good for the spiritual life of the asked, then it must be part of a holy disposition. So, what does this holy disposition, this ask-attitude look like?

First, a holy ask-attitude believes that every person in the church is gifted for meaningful service. Everyone in the church can excel in some kind of Spirit-gifted service. Paul told the church at Corinth that each one has a gift that makes plain the Holy Spirit for everyone's good (1 Cor 12:7–11). The Spirit shines in and through the gifts he's distributed in the community the Father has gathered. Scot McKnight puts it like this: "The healthiest, most vibrant churches are those in which each person's gift is exercised for the good of others, and each person is encouraged to use his or her gifts."[26] An ask-attitude requires a conviction that the Spirit can shine through anyone for the sake of the community.

Second, a holy ask-attitude recognizes the comic irony of who's doing the asking—so often in this case, the pastor. That God has called *this* person is a sign that God can place *any* in that position of modeling and leadership. That's the redemptive power of God's grace! It's OK for the pastor to have a little laugh at their own call to the pastorate, to be humbled at those who see the comedy of God's ways. It's good for leaders to have a friend or two for whom it's a hoot that God has placed them in leadership. Why? Because then the pastor will ask humbly, but also optimistically. A holy ask-attitude is humble, but also optimistic that God's grace can make good run deep in the believer and wild and wide through the believer.

Third, a holy ask-attitude asks with confidence. This isn't self-confidence but a confidence in God and the mission of God. Henri Nouwen says: "If this confident approach and invitation are lacking, then we [as leaders] are disconnected from our vision and have lost the direction of our mission."[27] There is honor in being asked to join in this mission. Ask in confidence that God is doing something important—and is even so gracious to do this work through us.

Let's explore this ask-attitude a little deeper. God chose and created humankind to be his image bearers. Further, God chose Israel as a kingdom of priests and holy nation for the whole world. God, from all eternity, chose his Son to be King and to embody this rule in Jesus of Nazareth. These claims aren't in competition with each other. God's affirmation that Jesus is King of Israel is also God's reaffirmed choice of Israel. And God's choice of Israel was the sign that God had not and will not give up on humankind. *It's in our bones to be chosen.* We *long* to be chosen, and only God's choice satisfies that longing. This means that when the pastor asks, the pastor is not asking from scratch. The ask comes within the context of God's having already chosen the person.

When pastors and leaders in the church remember that God has already chosen the person being asked, then a "No" is not necessarily a rejection of the pastor. Perhaps it is a "No" to God. Even when the pastor might suspect that the person asked is saying "No" to God, it is vital not to use these suspicions to prompt a change of mind. Instead, this should prompt the pastor to pray. Humility is necessary because perhaps the "No" to the pastor's request is actually a "Yes" to God and God's direction in the person's life.

But God's election doesn't just secure the asker when the answer is no. It also reminds the pastor and leader of the pastor's own security when the answer is yes. It is not the pastor's success that makes the pastor desirable to God; God desires fellowship with us simply because that's who God is. "Yes!" feels good, but it is only God's choice that satisfies the soul—every soul. Asking is not the route for the pastor or leader to feel satisfied;

it's a means for another to apply their satisfaction in Christ by serving in mission and in the church.

Healthy people like to be wanted. This is the overflow of election. If God desires us, then there is good in being rightly desired. If God chooses us, then there is good in being rightly chosen. Do you remember being chosen after a competitive job application process? Have you ever entered a competition and your performance or product was chosen for recognition? It feels good to be chosen! But election doesn't just mean God chooses us—and certainly not because of merit. God's election means that God doesn't *need* us. Christ needs no one; we need Christ. Healthy people like to be wanted, but unhealthy people too often like to be needed. Unhealthy people can manipulate or latch on tightly so that others think they are needed and necessary. Remember, asking is *never* begging. A holy ask-attitude of confidence is asking for help "standing up, not bowing down."[28]

A holy ask-attitude is relational and not transactional. Asking is about forming a relationship. Not every relationship is the same, but any time there's an ask, a relationship is implicit. Let me give you an example.

"Hey, can you fix my daughter's Kindle screen?" The shock of the shatter and the tears of my daughter made it so that the words were texted before I really thought about them. (Did you know that a misplaced knee displaces a Kindle's screen? Take my word for it.) "Maybe," came the reply. "How old is it?" Suddenly a host of factors popped into my mind. *How long would this task take? How much might it cost my friend in supplies he probably wouldn't charge me for? What if I could just buy a new Kindle for $50?* But then I realized something: I was willing to make this ask so quickly because this was my friend and I was okay inconveniencing his life and would be okay if he inconvenienced mine. I was free to make this request because of our friendship.

Every ask carries relational implications. If the request is simply transactional, then it's not a proper way to ask in ministry. If you are going to ask people to join in, they also must have a kind of implicit permission to ask you as well. Now, this doesn't mean you must always say yes—just as they have the freedom to say no. But anyone who dares ask must be open and accessible to being asked. Asking includes relationship.

Early in my ministry career, I noticed how easy it was to give a gift card or grocery voucher to a person with a purported need without caring about the relationship. In fact, I'm ashamed to admit, sometimes the gift card was a way of moving someone out of my office so that I could get back to my other tasks. But God's Spirit convicted me. A holy ask-attitude is about forming a relationship. As a result of God's conviction, listening, praying, brief encouragement, and counsel became a non-negotiable part of these kinds of conversations. And do you know what happened? I realized that, even though people sometimes asked the church for help without any interest in a relationship, I must still be relational whether or not the church was able to meet the need. I also realized that some people really, *really* wanted a relationship.

This reality can feel in tension with a common component of asking: the database, the list of names. If a ministry project, idea, or task is going to take ten people, you might draw up a list of twenty-five names. It is easy to make these lists based on percentage or to write names without thinking about them. A holy ask-attitude takes each person to heart. Take the opportunity to pray for those you ask before you make the ask. Focus on the "eachness" of the names rather than the "everyness" of the whole list.

Because asking is about relationship, it is a kind of ministry—both to be received and to be given. If this is the ask-attitude, then even if the answer is "No," asking remains ministry. The person has been asked to join the ministry and mission of Christ. What an honor! When you ask someone to make a commitment, to join, to participate, you are asking them to relate in a specific and potentially new and deeper way to Christ and Christ's mission. As a result, while asking can take energy, it shouldn't make us feel "tainted by unspiritual activity."[29] Asking is as spiritual as "giving a sermon, entering a time of prayer, visiting the sick, or feeding the hungry."[30]

Asking Environments

A consistent, holy ask-attitude is infectious. It is culture forming. When asking is faithful, humble, confident, and personal, then more people are willing to ask. And when more people are asking, more people are responding positively. You can multiply this personal disposition by developing an environment of asking. Here are two elements to keep in mind.

First, an automated system whereby people can self-select to sign up is vital. We don't know when the Spirit's nudge is ready to be received or when his nudge becomes a bit more like a shove. But when that happens, make sure people can respond and know how to respond! This might be a dedicated email address, an online form, or a section of perforated paper on the bulletin. If you have an automated system where people can respond to being asked, *follow up as soon as possible—and definitely not more than forty-eight hours later.* Do not simply use these systems to build a database. Why is quick and personal follow-up so important? Because if people volunteer but never get contacted, they can become cynical. If they get contacted too late, they may have cooled to their commitment. As a result, someone specific needs to oversee the system. If it isn't the pastor, then it needs to be another reliable person.

I was recently reminded of this truth—that automated systems are only as good as the data and personal follow-up—when I was in line at a crowded restaurant. After standing in line for about fifteen minutes to speak to the host, I put my name in for a party of eight. I was asked for my cell phone number and provided it, being told

I'd receive a text message in approximately fifteen minutes to confirm the table was ready. It was a loud environment, so I insisted on giving my number a second time, just to be safe. I was assured the text message would come. I waited fifteen minutes and no message came. I waited another five and went to check on things. Of course, you know what had happened. Some person, who was not me, had received a text message confirming their table was ready and had promptly deleted the message. When we have automated systems that are not followed up, it's like leaving a person waiting in line. Don't make people wonder if their data has been received and make sure that they are followed up with promptly and personally.

Second, keep ministry opportunities visible. People often don't see themselves doing something unless they see the thing they'll be doing. The physical structure of some churches is such that ministry opportunities are out of sight. Nurseries are hidden, classrooms are at the ends of long corridors, and so on. And what they say is true: out of sight, out of mind. By keeping ministries in sight, you're forming the imagination, giving space for God to spark ideas about good things running wild and wide and deep. Keep ministries and mission in mind through ministry fairs, testimonials, monthly highlights in the worship service, social media graphics and stories, and so on.

Conclusion

No chapter on asking would be complete without making a few final requests. So, here are my final requests of you.

Ask fast. Beth Seversen, author of *Not Done Yet: Reaching and Keeping Unchurched Emerging Adults*, notes that young adults want to get involved quickly.[31] The temptation is to give new attenders or new believers, perhaps especially young adults, a chance to settle in and become acquainted with a church before asking them to participate or to serve. Now, of course, you don't want to overwhelm people with incessant asking, and some roles require vetting that can only happen over time, but some roles can take new volunteers with simple background checks and a bit of good oversight. When my wife and I moved to Indiana, we knew we needed friends. On our second or third Sunday at our church, a family came up to us and asked us over for supper because we had mutual friends. "We understand you might need to get settled in before coming over." I piped up: "No, we can set a date. We're ready to connect with people." Serving alongside other people is one of the best ways to get connected at church and with God's people. Ask fast.

Ask again. Sometimes people said yes to me the first time. Sometimes they said no the first five times but yes on the sixth. There's a bit of an art form to asking. You can't ask incessantly, but you can ask persistently. Have you already asked someone, but they keep coming to mind? Perhaps there's a new role they could try. Ask again.

Ask personally. A personal tap on the shoulder works so much better than a general request. Yes, broad requests are necessary and sometimes helpful, but they are no substitute for personal invitations to serve. Ask personally.

Ask different people. Take a few moments and think about the kind of person you typically ask. Who are they? What are they like? What is their age? Their approximate income? Are they a man or a woman? Are they single or married? Do they work full-time, part-time, or are they retired? Are they a student? What is their education level? See if there is a pattern and, if there is, widen the group of people that you typically ask to join in or sign up.

Keep in mind that your asking systems will often pre-select who will sign up. For example, if your asking happens predominantly on Sunday mornings, then you have already limited your asking to people who are consistently in church. But sometimes serving is the route to people making corporate worship a priority. So have a variety of asking systems that will attract different people.

Ask selectively. I know this might go against the grain of some of this chapter, but when an opportunity or situation with significant risk or factors beyond your control is in play, ask selectively. If it is a person's first time serving and the stakes are relatively high—like a task force with a specific job to get done—then make sure they are properly overseen and supported in the role. If the stakes are a bit higher or there are elements beyond your control, then you might need to ask people who are likely to say yes, but whom you can also let down and who will allow you to ask them again.

Pastors need to be able to grow in the ability to ask. Asking is a ministry, an invitation to relationship, and a necessary part of lay leadership. But asking cannot be detached from knowing what help is being asked for, so let's turn our attention to ministry design.

CHAPTER 4

Task: Designing Fitting Roles and Responsibilities

Thank God for the "excellent absurdity" which enables us ... to play great parts without pride and little ones without dejection.

—C. S. Lewis

FWHIP, THUD; FWHIP, THUD; FWHIP, THUD. We had just heard the familiar squeak of snow beneath the tires late one evening, but this new sound wasn't so easily recognized. I hurried to the door and looked into the garage. A couple of unknown fellows were sliding stacks of newspapers across the flatbed of a truck and dropping them just inside the open garage door.

I opened the door and called out, "Whoa, whoa, whoa. I don't deliver this newspaper anymore." Apparently, these two new drivers had been given our address instead of the new carrier's. After delivering papers for about eighteen months, I had quit about a year earlier. Actually, maybe I only delivered papers for a month. It's hard to keep time straight when you're working the worst job you've ever had. Delivering newspapers by hand, carried in thick canvas bags slung over the shoulder, had resulted in many soaked feet, frozen hands, heavy eyelids, and an achy back. I wasn't about to let a fresh batch of papers be left in my garage.

"Do you want to deliver just these few bundles?" (People like to use diminutive adjectives when it comes to unpopular jobs they want you to do.) But I didn't like delivering papers, and I definitely didn't want to deliver them in the early morning dark of mid-winter doldrums.

Management experts and theologians agree: meaningless work is evidence of a world gone wrong. What a waste of talent! In a world full of ability, possibility, and responsibility, does it make sense for any work to be meaningless? In Genesis 1, human beings are described as the pinnacle of God's good creation and are given the mandate to be fruitful and multiply, to carry the order and beauty of Eden into the wider world. And in Ephesians 2, Paul doubles down on divine design by calling human beings God's craftsmanship, created in Christ Jesus to do good work.

While the first humans are described as coming at the end of God's design, we are more like Paul's commendation in Ephesians 2—caught right in the middle of God's work. Leadership can feel like building a plane while it's in the air. In Genesis 1, human beings wake up to their purpose in the world and the very next day is a day of rest because the creation is complete! And in Ephesians 2, human beings are told of their work in Christ Jesus, but it is Christ who has done what truly needs doing. We might say that meaningful work is redundant. Work highlights for human beings the tension of being unique but not essential. With these complementary affirmations, it's clear that leadership must both value work and have a sense of the task at hand to help people sort out their work in Christ so that good can run wild in the church, wide in the world, and deep in the believer.

Know the Task Being Asked

"So, what is it that you want me to do—like, specifically?"

About forty-five minutes into a conversation where I was being recruited for a volunteer position, I still didn't have an answer. I was told why I would be good at the role; I was told why the role would benefit my wider life; I was told why the role was necessary. I just didn't know what the role involved.

Neither did the recruiter.

I have been that recruiter from time to time. My pastoral ministry has included moments of pitching and inviting and recruiting to jobs, roles, responsibilities, and tasks that I didn't really understand.

There was a day in the church when the job title communicated everything you needed to know about the job. People could fill in the details seamlessly. If the volunteer didn't know what to do, their aunt, uncle, cousin, neighbor, or pew-mate did. But that day has gone. Willing volunteers don't always know what goes into a role. And the natural support network is no longer so common. What makes this even more challenging is that the pastor doesn't always know the role, either. In the wider work world, job titles only work when people know what they mean. Sometimes a job title is crystal clear within a specific field but clear as mud to anyone on the outside. Changes in worship styles, demographics, family systems, and technology mean that job titles in church contexts not only carry less meaning, but many people feel like outsiders to the jobs.

After that conversation ended with no answer to my question, I realized that the previous volunteer needed replacing because they didn't know what to do, either. I didn't take the volunteer job. Whenever someone is asked but there isn't clarity on the role, then all the courage it took to make the ask is just wasted energy. You've got to know what you're asking someone to do.

Begin knowing a task by analyzing what it takes to do it well. Every leader must have a sense of the work that others under their leadership are asked to do. This doesn't mean the pastor or lay leader must be an expert in the task, but they must have sense of what the task requires:

- appropriate passions/interests
- skills and abilities (oral or written communication, technological skills

like sound or social media, lifting or other physical activity)

- competencies (leadership, motivation, problem-solving)
- personality (self-initiating, detail-oriented, introversion/extraversion)
- experience (including spiritual maturity)
- knowledge (of the local church, of the local community, theology, Bible)
- time commitment and rhythm

Leaders also must know when the task is complete. This might be a schedule or a set of details to complete before the task is done. This aspect of ministry is important for two, perhaps opposite, reasons. First, it is important to know when the task is complete so that the person will go home! Some volunteers just can't seem to stop. They might even take overworking as a sign of faith and loyalty to God. They always find another detail to handle and job to do. I have watched weary children get lugged from room to room in the church because the volunteer, their parent, didn't quite know when to stop. Remember: we are serving God in ministry; we are not serving the false god of ministry. Too many children have been sacrificed to the idol of ministry because of unclear expectations. Second, it is important to know when the task is complete so that the person doesn't leave prematurely. I wound sound cables incorrectly only once because someone taught me how to do it properly. Just as nothing is more frustrating than unpacking a snake-like tangle of sound cables, so is hardly anything so demoralizing in ministry as coming into a dirty room or searching through unsorted supplies. The last responsibilities of the task are vital to setting up the next ministry. If the leader doesn't know what goes into a faithful and complete accomplishment of the task—both so that it comes to an end and sets up the next beginning—then it is unclear.

Knowing the task is not the same as making it rigid or unchanging. Knowing the task means providing freedom for input, tweaks, and insights from the person doing the work. People want to play a role in figuring out aspects of the role or responsibility. Such input affirms that volunteers and laity are people in a community, not pegs punched into a (job) board. Seth Godin illustrates this perfectly by telling the story of Betty Crocker's initial failure on its famous cake mix. At first, all the eager cake consumer needed to do was add water and pop the mix into the oven. But it turns out that purchasers wanted to play a bigger role—even with their pre-packaged food. So, what did Betty Crocker do? They changed the recipe so that the purchaser needed to add an egg and oil. Now the buyer felt like a baker![32] The leader who knows the task will be able to receive more input regarding the task so that the volunteer can play a larger role in its design.

Teams, Task Forces, Committees, and Councils

The task will also have a natural make-up of personnel, but they should all emphasize teamwork and teams. Early in my ministry, I was struggling to recruit and train greeters. Greeters are so important in the life of the church because they are the first face many will see—perhaps the very first face seen in church. Greeters disarm the tension of a young family that hurried to get out the door and had a spat in the van; greeters offer a supportive arm and hold the door for the senior; greeters make sure people know where to take their children if there's separate programming. I knew how important greeters were, but I was failing in building the team. Then I made a *critical* error: I redesigned the ministry to require fewer people. My logic was sound, but terribly misguided: If I'm struggling to get twelve people, maybe I'll just recruit six. Bad move. I lost some of those six. Only then did I realize that, if someone is good at greeting, they might want to be around people. Some ministries don't need *fewer* ministers doing *more* work with lower expectations. Instead, they might need *more* people doing *less* work but with higher expectations. Sometimes people need a teammate. Teams carry natural potential, a kind of hidden power. Try doubling the number of people needed in a role and seeing if the fellowship makes a difference. Allow more of the body of Christ to serve in ministry and see if there's momentum. Don't neglect the potential of teams. The body of Christ is, after all, a *body*. Now, this doesn't mean that all tasks need to be done in tandem, but there should always be a connection with others in the ministry.

Beyond the philosophy of teams, a task might have three different kinds of groups. While the words might be used differently in your context, I find the following breakdown helpful:

- Task forces are time-sensitive teams with a clear mandate. Once the job is done, it is disbanded, but hopefully with increased familiarity, momentum, and potential for future work.
- Committees are ongoing teams with a specific range of responsibility that outlives the service of the members.
- Councils are ongoing teams that give oversight from a higher vantage point that addresses wider concerns.

Accept Duties, Avoid Drudgeries, and Design for Delight

I think of tasks falling into three categories: duties, drudgeries, and delights. Remember from last chapter that everyone is gifted to excel in some area of service. When we are serving in areas of effectiveness, it is often a *delight*. People enjoy being competent at something that matters. Along the way, certain tasks might also become *duties*.

Just like my children have duties simply by being part of the family, so there are certain tasks that come with being part of the church. What needs to be avoided is *drudgery*. Now, there are some tasks that many people would like to do and there are some tasks that only a few people would like to do. If there are tasks that need to be done but no one is willing, then it might be a sign that this is a job for hire rather than an opportunity for ministry. The task might require a certain amount of time, expertise, flexibility, or something else to be done well.

So, how can tasks be more about delight than duty? By *design*. Think again about Paul's word in Ephesians 2: workmanship. Human beings are not something thrown together with leftover bits of material, a mere afterthought of a busy maker. We are created in Christ, who is the very begotten of the Father. We are part of God's design. As a result, leaders must also be careful that ministry maintains its character, its stamp, its image—as work to be done by those made in the image of God. Ministry is always Christ serving graciously in and through those under his leadership. Our work in Christ should aim to match the beauty of God's workmanship revealed in the workers God has made.

Design can turn duties into delights. When leaders delegate duties simply because they are duties they'd rather not do, then trust can be strained and morale can suffer. No one wants to sign up for a task only to hear, "I'm glad you're doing this. Now I don't have to do it." See the craftsmanship of the Creator in the person you're leading and apply your creativity and design to the task being formed. Duties turn into delights when intentionally connected with such faith-features as fellowship, spirituality, purpose, and relationships.

So, how can we go about ministry design? There are any number of examples of design processes. If you're familiar with design processes, then you might already have your own system. If you do, then I strongly suggest reflecting on it, writing it down, and analyzing it objectively to see how it might be improved or taught to others. If you aren't familiar with design process, then familiarize yourself with one model and follow it. Only after you've tried it out a few times should you tweak and modify it. It's never foolish to let the experience of another be your starting point! Here's a potential design system.[33]

Identify a need. Did you know that empathy is a human superpower?[34] Human beings are hardwired to empathize with others through the growth and development of mirror neurons. We can also grow in this ability to identify another's emotions and to share in their painful experiences. Allow empathy to spark your awareness of existing needs in your church and community. You can also gather data from congregants via surveys or by delving into email requests from the last year. On one occasion I preached a sermon on God meeting needs. As a way of responding, I listed a handful of needs on a slip of paper, distributed the papers to the congregation, and invited the congregation to identify which they had and to bring them before the Lord anonymously. Some of the needs were only ones that God could provide mysteriously and even miraculously, but some of the needs God could meet through the church!

Needs might also be conceived as opportunities. What opportunities exist to do something beautiful, symbolic, or otherwise gospel-oriented? Recall that leadership is seeing. Allow your spiritual eye to spot opportunities in the church and community. Nothing supports seeing like taking time simply to be present in the church's body life and the culture of the wider community.

Brainstorm possibilities that address the need or seize an opportunity. Needs are notoriously difficult, layered, and complex. Meeting immediate needs is sometimes a bit like remodeling the eleventh floor of a building whose foundation needs repair. Does that mean it shouldn't be done? No, remodeling can make a difference—but doing good must not become a distraction from wider needs. As you generate possibilities, there is a blend of being practical, avoiding unintended harm, and refraining from despair. When we recognize that needs are complex, we will be careful to avoid doing harm. When we see needs that can be met, we will be humble in doing good. When we stay close to God, we are in the only place to avoid despair at the world's needs and instead to be filled with hope at God's good future.

C. S. Lewis said that the *Chronicles of Narnia* all started with the image of a faun carrying some packages with an umbrella in a snowy wood. For Brenda, a vision for a ministry started a little less fantastically: "I've got an extra freezer," she told me. I had chatted with Brenda many times, but she was probably never so to-the-point. And just like that, a ministry was born. It wasn't yet designed, but the vision for a small food pantry was sparked.

Eventually, the vision blossomed into a small pantry with basic non-perishable items, and the aforementioned freezer was stocked with labeled meals for families in grief and need.

When just beginning to generate ideas, don't ask too many "how" questions. Let an idea get at least semi-formed before testing its applicability. Nothing kills an idea faster than asking, "How?" repeatedly. Many ideas have been prematurely dismissed with questions like:

- How are we going to pay for it?
- How are we going to get enough volunteers?
- How will the room get set up?
- How will it all get cleaned up?

Experiment with the idea. Experiments aren't about winning or losing. They are about finding something out. Experiments help leaders to find out what they don't yet know. Experiments let leaders know whether ideas are sustainable; whether tasks take unique talent or specific skill previously unknown; whether or not ideas require more personnel or allow for more self-direction or, instead, more management; whether the ministry idea needs more flexibility or greater training. Experiments need a bit of control, though; they are ways to test an idea before implementing it more widely. Think of ministry experiments as akin to dress rehearsals or restaurants opening to family and friends.

When experimenting, allow the creativity to continue. One of the most fun aspects of design and innovation is placing opposites together. We bring together concepts that have no relation or we weave stories that are otherwise distinct. Think about how so many fairy tales or fables bring together two opposites, like naïve children and wily witches or a big bad wolf and a little girl in a red tunic or rabbits and turtles. Remakes of old stories also provide twists: Shrek is *not* the handsome prince but the ogre whose princess-bride becomes an ogre as well. Ministry design also gives an opportunity to innovate by bringing different things together. Try these practices with existing ministries or with new ideas in the experimentation phase.[35]

Place the idea in a different context. "What would this look like in a nursing home?" Mandy asked. A group of us were brainstorming a ministry project with Mandy's support. I paused. "Um ... it wouldn't work" was my first thought. But then I asked myself, "Well, why wouldn't it work?" and I realized that I had placed unnecessary restrictions on the idea without knowing it. If you have an idea, try placing it in different contexts to see what sparks. What might this look like on a military base? Or before a minor league baseball game? Could it happen in a restaurant?

Play the idea out with different characters. What if all the volunteers were teenage girls? Or retired teachers? Or single dads? Sam, a friend of mine from a large church on the West Coast, was leading a greeting ministry. Sam was a single dad of two daughters. He knew the stresses and strains of single-parenting and loved being a lay leader in his church. So, he put them together. He targeted single dads as greeters. Now, they weren't the only participants in this ministry, but they provided enough support that the ministry took on a new life because they knew what information, communication, or opportunities that brand new guests needed in the church. It also became a ministry to single dads because of the support that was provided.

Plan the idea out with different calendars. Put the idea in summer or fall. Think about what it might mean to practice it strictly during Advent or Lent.

What if it was to coincide with the Super Bowl, Stanley Cup, or World Series? Instead of gathering weekly for 7 weeks a small group could meet each night of a playoff series. Or have a fellowship event during the first two afternoons of March Madness basketball. Saturday night services work for shift workers and Sunday coaches.

Pray the idea out with different churches. Depending on your geographic location and denomination, this may or may not be important or even an opportunity. Frankly, churches can become very proprietary with their ideas. I get it. And it really, really hurts to have someone steal your idea—especially if they have a bigger budget. Church competition is real and it's ugly. Instead of competing, ask how this idea can reflect the abundance of God. Sometimes we need to risk sharing ideas with other church leaders in a spirit of camaraderie and prayer and openhandedness. What will God do with such generosity and sharing? Asking questions like this reminds us that new ideas are right around the corner. Indeed, this sharing may well be sanctifying. After all, leadership in ministry is not about being known by the church, but the Lord making himself known through the church.

Mobilize for more experiments. Mobilization is about widening the ministry or idea in light of what you've found out in the experiment. But what you've found out in the experiment isn't obvious. There is still a mystery to be solved, and it requires some analysis. Before replicating the idea, the leader needs to find out why something worked. Was it the personnel? Was there a single person who was the secret sauce? Was it the timing? Did it work because there was so much momentum? Some experiments work because the followers are so invested that they won't let it fail, but this kind of commitment isn't sustainable. It is easy to sense the success of an event, a ministry idea, a new role, etc., and simply ascribe it to the mysteries of God, believing that God's blessing will continue. Of course the experiment holds a measure of mystery—press into it! Analyze and discuss what made it work or what God used to make it work.

This means continuing to experiment by applying what has been found out. *Keep (almost) everything an experiment.* If (almost) everything is an experiment, then there is always permission to learn and grow from mistakes.

Replicate responsibly. This final component usually involves some kind of systematizing. Design without replicability is incomplete, but it is important to remember that systems exist to serve, not to be served. In systems theory, hierarches in systems exist to serve lower-order systems. For example, children do not exist to fulfill parents; rather, parents exist for children to flourish. Schools and hospitals and businesses don't exist to support government; no, government exists to facilitate education, health, and commerce. However, both higher and lower can forget their place.[36] When a person begins to think and act like their role is more important than the ministry as a whole, or when a ministry begins to think it is more important than the church as a whole, then the lower-order system has forgotten its place. This is called suboptimization. Likewise, when there is too much control from the top, lower-order systems cannot develop resilience or self-organization. The higher has forgotten its purpose.

There are always tensions around replication—expedience vs. quality vs. cost; systematization vs. personalization. Ministry is both simple and complex. Some of these tensions cannot be avoided. What can be avoided are unnecessary roadblocks. Apply resources to remove obstacles and to simplify work.

I'll give an example. A growing ministry was a hit. It had identified a need, generated possibilities, experimented, and mobilized for more insight. So, the pastor went to replicate the ministry on a consistent basis. However, as it was replicated, it simply didn't have enough personnel. Volunteers were moved from another ministry that the pastor oversaw to cover the shortage. Unfortunately, this roadblock of insufficient personnel was never addressed in the replication phase. By conscripting volunteers from across other ministries, the pastor left other ministry leaders frustrated and volunteers confused.

Conclusion

The best plans fail. The strongest designs disintegrate. There are unintended consequences. There are misplaced resources and missed opportunities. Moreover, there is an enemy who attempts to thwart our plans. How strange, then, when the quickest plans succeed and spontaneous designs bear fruit! Allow Psalm 108 to become common in your ministry meetings: "With God we will gain the victory, and he will trample down our enemies" (Ps 108:13). Because *God* has conquered our foes, what valiant work we can do! "Commit your work to the Lord, and your plans will be established" (Prov 16:3 NRSV). And may Peter's words dwell in your heart: "Humble yourselves therefore under the mighty hand of God, so that he may exalt you in due time. Cast all your anxiety on him, because he cares for you" (1 Pet 5:6–7).

CHAPTER 5

Train: Equipping People for Ministry

So Christ himself gave the apostles, the prophets, the evangelists, the pastors and teachers, to equip his people for works of service.

—Ephesians 4:11–12

CHRIST PROVIDES LEADERS IN THE CHURCH TO equip the people for ministry so that the body of Christ may be built up into unity and knowledge and maturity, achieving the fullness of Christ (Eph 4:11–13). Whew! That's quite a mouthful. But notice the connection between spiritual formation and ministry. Ministry and ministry *preparation* lead to fullness in Christ. Paul says that leaders are provided for the *equipping* of the people. Especially in the context of the care of souls, training the laity in ministry and leadership is not simply meant to check items off a list, capture a signature on a waiver, or fulfill insurance requirements. No, ministry training that cares for the soul must be about forming the soul.

Ministry training is spiritual formation. This is so because ministry itself is spiritual formation. As the Holy Spirit graciously disciplines our embodied lives through faithful practices, the Holy Spirit forms and empowers the human spirit to direct and move the body in loving service, or ministry. Of course, it is Christ's interest in us that inspires our service to him. Ministry training that is spiritual formation may begin with our initial, superficial interest. But it must go deeper.

I recall what started as a friendly meal around the table turned into a passionate imparting of my host's pastime. After dinner, I was anticipating a bit of conversation before I excused myself. I was youngish, unmarried, and eager to take in a movie with some friends. But I never made it to the movie. Instead, I learned more than I knew it was possible to learn about trains. I heard about routes, freight and shipping, track width, and standardized time.

I was also shown a model train—one that my gracious and talented host had built. It had been appraised at approximately half my annual salary. The detail, care, and attention given to the model was inspiring. For that evening, anyway, I was captured by trains. My host's interest was infectious. Too often, when ministry training ignores the deeper work of spiritual formation—of caring for souls by forming souls—then the connection lasts not much longer than one brief season of ministry.

My host needed passion to engage my interest, but passion wasn't enough. The leader *must* bring a measure of passion and commitment to the training. Ministry training is sharing and supporting in the mutual interest of the ministry of Jesus Christ by the power of the Holy Spirit. As Paul told Philemon, "I pray that your partnership with us in the faith may be effective in deepening your understanding of every good thing we share for the sake of Christ" (Phlm 6).

Basic Training

Because ministry training is spiritual formation, the ultimate end remains the same for every person being trained: Christlikeness. God is committed to seeing Christ formed in all who are in

Christ by sanctifying their unique identities. We are all one in Christ and we will all be like Christ, yet we will all be unique persons in Christ, too, to the glory of God.

Every person being trained for ministry and formed for Christlikeness will have a unique makeup of skills (hands), passions (heart), and intellect (head). And ministry training can focus on each:

- Train the hands: What does a person need to be able to do?
- Train the heart: What does the person need to be able to appreciate or to feel?
- Train the head: What does the person need to know? How do they need to be able to reason?
- Train in habits: What habits will spark and sustain spiritual growth?[37]

All people should be challenged to continue growing. There must be appropriate, not overwhelming, challenge for those serving in ministry. Everyone's hands, heart, and head can grow in love toward God and be submitted to his service in Christ by the Spirit. Leadership expert Ken

Blanchard has said that a great job is made up of approximations.[38] The church is full of people who can do a great job by being close enough, knowing when close enough doesn't cut it, and when their leaders help them to get a bit closer to the mark.

Of course, just as not all ministry tasks and responsibilities require the same skills, passions, or imaginations, so not all people have the same capacities, interests, and abilities. While it is wise to help people grow in areas where they are naturally strong, each capacity is a gift from God and should be developed as an act of worship. Yet in spite of difference, when we keep spiritual formation the focus of ministry training, *every* stretch, *every* bit of growth, *every* approximation achieved is an act of worship and a context for God's transforming grace. Even as we talk about the ministry system and why training is an important part of leadership formation, we must always remember that ministry and ministry training—the whole process—is about creating little Christs.[39]

Missing the Train

Precisely because ministry training is spiritual formation, there are subtle reasons pastors avoid training the laity. First, spiritual formation doesn't happen in a hurry. The church community is beautifully distinguished from the corporate world by allowing training to be *inefficient*—we invest time in someone because we care for *who they are* more than *what they can do.* Of course, we don't want to waste resources in training, but we want to be aware that human beings are the most important "resources" in ministry. If they are built up in Christ by forming their spiritual lives, deepening their relationships, and expanding their hearts, then there is no waste. Instead, there are eternal effects. When ministry training is spiritual formation, it doesn't stop. Some training sessions should take place only after a season of ministry to allow the people being trained to draw on their experiences as case studies with opportunities and problems to be addressed.

Second, training will bring us into difficult conversations with those being trained. After all, spiritual formation is deeply connected with discipline. In the illustration above, my host's passion for trains only increased his appreciation for planning, precision, detail, effectiveness, and efficiency as it came to trains and their operation. Ministry training desires all the same things, even if efficiency takes on a different meaning in spiritual formation.

Third, the one being trained isn't the only one being formed. Just as Christ's teaching was to complete his disciples' joy, so may the pastor's teaching, *because it is Christ teaching*, be a source of joy for the pastor, too (John 15:11). But what a risk! Training will reveal the trainer's own spiritual needs. It is hard—even hypocritical—to teach on habits if the leader isn't practicing them. There's a famous story about Gandhi and a boy's desperate mother. She wanted the boy to stop eating sugar. Nothing she had tried helped. Finally, she brought her son to the great leader, pleading, "Tell my son to stop eating sugar!" Seeing the passion in the mother's face, Gandhi replied, "Come back in one year." Confused but willing, the mother left, returning one year later, her son in tow. Gandhi looked at the boy and said, "Young man, you must stop eating sugar." Grateful but somewhat confused, the mother said, "Thank you, sir! Thank you! But may I ask why you didn't tell him this one year ago?" Gandhi quietly replied, "Because I needed to stop eating sugar, myself, before I could tell another to do so." Of course, if the pastor and spiritual leader is also a learner, then they can admit to learning what they are teaching. But you must be open to accountability. You do not always need to have mastered what you are teaching, but you do need to be diligent in learning. Allow Christ to continue teaching you to complete your joy.

While I learned a lot of content about trains throughout that evening and into the night, I also learned a lesson about teaching: teachers who love their subjects are infectious teachers. If you've lost the passion for ministry, it will show up in ministry training. And nothing reveals lost passion more than just *not doing the training.* Because ministry training is spiritual formation, the trainer must not only be devoted to forming others but to being formed personally, as well. There is no other option for the church's leaders who train others for ministry. The trainer must be devoted to the One in whose name ministry is being done.

Fourth, ministry training can reveal the state of the trainer's influence. If people don't consider the event necessary, they won't attend. Without the influence of the leader, they'll opt out. And if they don't show up, the leader might not have the influence they think they should.

Sadly, I didn't realize that ministry training is spiritual formation very early in my ministry. I took people through too many sessions where, graciously and without my intent, the Spirit showed up and people left different than when they came in. Too many times I focused solely on skills and not on the human spirit. I also trained too little. I worried I was burdening people or wouldn't get the commitment, and so I let myself off the training hook. If ministry training isn't spiritual formation, then we will not train enough and we will not address the spiritual life of the believer. But when ministry training is spiritual formation, then it doesn't matter if the group is one, ten, or a hundred. Spiritual formation happens in groups of various sizes, so training can take different approaches. Consider small group contexts, or even one-on-one training times.

All Aboard!

Ministry training involves onboarding—bringing people into an active ministry role intentionally. Picture someone part on, part off the train, running at its side, trying to catch it before it accelerates to top speed. Or a passenger standing on the platform, unsure if they want to go on the trip. When someone isn't properly onboarded, it's like they're left holding on by just a foot or finger. Inevitably, they fall off—and painfully.

A good onboarding process attends to three contexts: organizational, technical, and social.[40] Organizational onboarding means becoming familiar with day-to-day (or week-to-week) rhythms, definitions and "insider" language, flow of information, appropriate history, what the organization thinks is important (its values), what the organization assumes (its norms), and what the organization is about (its mission). Technical onboarding means developing appropriate skills with the various tools and available resources (including technology) and ways of doing things (processes). Finally, social onboarding means knowing the interpersonal expectations of a given ministry and having a network of people—friends and acquaintances—within the organization. *Everyone* needs to be a *someone* to someone else. If you, as the leader, are the one person that other people know, then they will only have a sliver of your time and connection on a Sunday morning (or whenever the ministry is taking place). When Jethro taught Moses to delegate to other trustworthy men, it wasn't only to protect Moses. It was to serve the people. Cases were ruled and so community continued (Exod 18:17–26).

If any of these aspects is missing, then someone's left with a foot dragging behind while the train picks up speed. They might keep up for a bit, but eventually they'll be flung from the car. Here's what happens when one of the aspects is not there.

When there is organizational onboarding and social onboarding but no technical onboarding, there is an *incompetent insider.* While on board with the organization's goals and lingo and history, and part of a network of people, the incompetent insider lacks the necessary skills to contribute. They're inside but they're not able to make key contributions. Either they feel it, or others do. Technical skills might include writing emails with a relational tone, greeting people warmly, organizing curriculum, bringing order to a crowd, drawing up a budget, exegeting Scripture. Technical onboarding might include technological skills. This is especially precipitous in a technological age because while some are native to technology, it can intimidate other people. And intimidated people do not feel cared for. And people who do not feel cared for are at risk of losing, or abusing, their social connections, too. Whatever skills are needed in the role should be considered in the training.

When there is organizational onboarding and technical onboarding but no social onboarding, then there is a *skilled loner.* The skilled loner is on board with the organization and they've got the required skills, but they're doing things by themselves. They show up, deliver, and sneak away. Or, worse, they stand around waiting to be known but nobody really knows them. This is a tricky bit of onboarding because people want different levels of connection. Some may even want a season of anonymity. Their relational quota to feel on board might be lower than others. Another tricky situation is the person or family who has been around a long time. Other people know their name(s) and, as a result, they are assumed to be known. They might even be a person or family that has welcomed others. But inside, they feel isolated and alone. They do not feel connected. Everyone—whether they desire few or many relationships—needs meaningful relationships in ministry.

Finally, when there is technical onboarding and social onboarding but no organizational onboarding, then there is a *misaligned member.* Interpersonal relationships and valuable skills are present, but the sense of belonging in the organization is missing. This can come across as though the person is holding something back, always offering a half-hearted commitment. Service in ministry might be off and on. They offer ministry ideas that never quite seem to fit with the church's mission. Weak organizational onboarding might result in a tension with theological positions or confusion with organizational structure or just a deficit in familiarity with the organization.

Take a few minutes and try to name the lay leaders that you count on. Who do you contact in a pinch? Now start moving outward. Who do you contact when the key people are unavailable? The goal isn't to name all the laity involved in ministry and mission. It is to name those with whom you have significant influence and who see you as a leader. Are they onboarded? Do they have a leg that's dragging or are they running to catch the train? Who needs help onboarding right now? Which onboarding angle might be lacking (organizational, technical, social)? If you can name it, you can do something about it.

Now take it a step further. What do you need to get on board or to stay on board? Sadly, some pastors run for months, even years, to keep up with the train but never fully feel they've climbed aboard. What would keep you aboard? Think about having a meaningful conversation with the right people before turning in a resignation letter or asking for a new placement. It is also helpful to have other leaders do the same exercise. They might even ask to meet with you to feel more on board.

One overlooked bit of training that influences each area is the ability to offer an apology and to express forgiveness. The church is a community of sinners who have received forgiveness and for whom not forgiving others is not an option. Knowing how to receive God's conviction, express sorrow, and receive forgiveness can be a unique training for the church.

C.A.B.L.E. Cars

Cable cars run along railways by gripping and releasing a constantly moving cable. When the cable is gripped, the car is moving. When the cable is released, the car stops. Chapters 2, 3, and 4 have been about the mechanism that helps the car to grip the cable. *Casting* vision, *asking f*or commitment, and designing *tasks* are all geared to help the "car" latch on to something to get moving. But without the moving cable, cars stay where they are. Ministry training is the moving cable. If someone catches the vision, signs up for a role, and responds to the ask, but they don't have any training, then they won't be moving. And just as the cable should keep moving, likewise ministry training must be ongoing in the church's rhythm. Training must be a consistent element of the whole ministry and leadership system.

Ongoing ministry training is necessary because we can forget the overall purpose. People might get invigorated for a season but then lose interest or change schedules or find another ministry. Yet, if there is ongoing training, then the "cars" will have made progress through the spiritual formation of ministry training. Remember: training is never simply for the task. In the church, ministry training is spiritual formation—it is care for the soul.

Consistent ministry training should include the C.A.B.L.E.:

- Commonalities in the church's ministries
- Available support
- Best practices and policies
- "Living" schedule
- Emergency actions and measures

Commonalities. Ask what is common across the whole church or is needed for everyone in a specific ministry. First, the faith is common. Every person involved in ministry who has a personal faith in Jesus Christ must be trained to share the gospel of Jesus Christ personally and to share their personal testimony. Ministry training is a wonderful time to tell the story of Jesus and his saving work. But what about people who are serving in ministry but haven't yet made a personal commitment or don't have a personal faith? What an opportunity for them to hear the testimony of a peer. What a moment for them to have a chance to respond to the gospel. Pastors must seek to train every person in ministry to share the gospel.

Second, what is the church's mission and what are the church's core values? Every training gathering is a chance to reinforce the "why" and the "what's important." It's a chance to cast vision and reinforce values. By expressing the church's mission and values publicly, not only will the laity be informed and aware, but they can also provide accountability. Encourage a culture of transparency and questions. Values shouldn't simply be verbal commitments in training sessions but practical guides in ministry settings.

Third, what are the common hopes you have for every volunteer and lay leader? How do these hopes connect to the spiritual formation of each volunteer? As Andy Stanley has said, it is important for people to know what their leaders want *for* them before they know what they want *from* them.[41] Remind people what you want for them personally as they serve and lead in ministry. If a layperson experiences different values and treatment between different ministries, then you need to examine what values and hopes are being communicated and to bring ministries back into alignment with the whole church.

Fourth, what will the ministry activity typically be like? What can be expected? Is there a schedule, rhythm, or routine? The rhythm might be daily, seasonal, and/or yearly. What patterns exist that can also support the spiritual life of the person?

Fifth, address common problems. When I was training small group leaders, I covered two topics consistently: the length of meetings and the lending of money. Nothing threatened to disrupt a small group like going too long or asking other members for a loan. And it seemed that every group faced at least one of these challenges. What problems consistently come up in the ministry you're leading?

Train lay leaders with simple solutions. Addressing common problems is like removing small obstacles from the track. Small obstacles can keep the largest engines from moving.

Available support. Who do I contact if something goes wrong? Who can I tell if something goes right? Who will help me sort out when I'm not quite sure? Who will unlock a door, find me a markerboard, or help with an upset child? Hopefully there aren't three different answers. It is always helpful to give partners, volunteers, and sponsors a single point of contact. Now, this might not always be possible, but limiting the amount of people one needs to contact across various scenarios is very helpful. When someone isn't quite sure who to contact, they will often contact more than one person. For example, a scheduling question might spark an email or a text message to a church administrator, a pastor, a friend, and a church-answer-person. The result can be duplicated work, mixed messaging, unhelpful advocacy, and still no clear answer. Providing a single point of contact can also highlight, painfully, how vital only one or two people have become to too many people. If only one or two people have all the necessary information, knowledge, or power, then there are unnecessary bottlenecks in the ministry system. And they might be sick of being the single point of contact for too many people.

Best practices and policies. "Pastor Aaron, when you talk to children, try getting down on a knee and being at their level." I had six years of formal ministry training, and I was about to enter informal, "on the job" ministry training. And that bit of wisdom was exactly what I needed. I started being more intentional in how I spoke, not only with children but with adults as well. Every person desires to do a job well. If someone signs up for a job, they want to do it effectively. Even if they decide it's not the right fit, they want to make that decision for themselves, not to be told the decision has been made for them.

This story also reminds me that pastors are not experts in every ministry. A caring lay leader pointed this out to me when I was supposed to be training them. Ministry training doesn't mean always being the expert; it means finding the right teachers, the "content experts," who are often right in the church. An added benefit to the laity being models for other laity in ministry is that it undermines the temptation to professionalize ministry itself—as though *only* the pastor does ministry right and everybody else is just filling in. When ministry training is spiritual formation, then the whole church can be involved in the training.

Training includes explaining policies, including ethical policies, security policies, social media policies, financial policies, and so on. However, be careful with the creation of policies because they can have unintended consequences. Here's what so often happens. A challenging situation comes up and it's a mess to deal with. There are hurt feelings and unnecessary departures. Naturally, we never want the situation to happen again, so we develop a policy to keep it from happening. When we make policies in a reactive mode, the policy is often either too rigid, too flexible, too specific, or too broad. It has a loophole. Common sense demands it be broken at some point. And so the policy is ignored or sporadically enforced. And then, over time, people start to become bored with policies or, worse, cynical toward them: "Well, if that rule doesn't really matter, then perhaps this one doesn't, either." People might notice that only some policy breakers are being held accountable. And now the policy isn't making things simpler; it's making them more complex. There's a mess and hurt feelings and an unnecessary departure—followed by the writing of a new policy.

Ministry will always have challenging situations. It will always have complexities that need to be addressed. As much as we wish they would, policies simply don't eliminate complex situations. Policies do not serve to keep us from complexity, but to provide basic simplicity when things are complex. This doesn't mean we shouldn't have any policies, but that we should follow some guidelines when developing them. I find these "rules about the rules" helpful:

1. If you don't need a policy, don't make one.
2. If you need a policy, make it clear, precise, and limited because you don't know what unintended consequences it will have.
3. Enforce the policy consistently with minimalist consequences.
4. Evaluate policies when the need arises and on a regular schedule (not more than annually).

And remember that nobody attends ministry training because they're excited to hear about policies.

In addition to policies, training should also include what are often called "best practices." Best practices are just good ways of doing things when there might be several options. An example is the practice I noted earlier of getting down to a child's level to speak with them. That bit of investment has paid off exponentially. I love focusing on best practices because, if a person breaks a policy, there has to be accountability. If a person doesn't follow a best practice, then we just keep on teaching. It gets reinforced or a better way is discerned. People might even wisely go against custom or precedent from time to time. Now, of course, if a person keeps ignoring the ongoing training and the guidance of their leaders, then there's another problem. But focusing on best practices and limiting policies reduces much of the peril of policies.

Best practices encourage wisdom and ownership. People eventually find their own way of doing things that strengthens the ministry. When people have a sense of responsibility and a measure of autonomy to bring their own self and ideas to a ministry, there is greater learning and ownership.

In leadership studies, this is called self-determination theory. Now, different people might need to start at different levels. Some people might need more best practices, more specific ways of doing things until they have enough experience to engage in ministry with a bit more personal style. Training in practices is meant to build competence ("I know what needs to be done and I know when it is being done well"), confidence ("I can do this"), and freedom ("I can try something new"). These factors are needed in different amounts at different times. Knowing the people serving in ministry and how they can take greater ownership and where they need to grow is a non-negotiable part of leadership. This is part of knowing your flock, knowing your people. Ministry training is spiritual formation.

"Living" schedule. Every volunteer, sponsor, and ministry partner needs to know about the schedule—including how to break it. They need a measure of stability and predictability, but also autonomy and flexibility. This means the schedule is "live," which involves two factors. First, the expectations of the leaders and the role should be clearly communicated, especially if the role requires more stability. Second, people need to know the best time and way to make changes to

the schedule. Depending on the complexity of the ministry, people might be able to make changes themselves to a schedule that lives online. Or they might need to inform a ministry administrator.

Schedules have chronic tension. Ministry partners, sponsors, and volunteers will have unexpected opportunities that prompt them to cancel, even at a moment's notice. It might feel like unreliability, but it also might just be a person's spontaneous nature. Leaders need to develop an ability to handle the chronic tension that comes from last-minute changes. If you have spontaneous people, they will call things off. It's frustrating. It would be worse if you didn't have any spontaneous people, because they are often energetic and bring life to the ministry.

Emergency actions and measures. I was about six years old when our region implemented 9-1-1. We were trained thoroughly and consistently what to do in case of an emergency: Dial 9-1-1. It was on the television; it was in school; my parents taught me. About twenty years later, as I entered a shopping mall, a stranger began having a seizure right in front of me. It was a scary event. My first instinct was as foolish as it was natural. Looking down at the distressed individual, I asked, "Do you want me to call 9-1-1?" Fortunately, my childhood training kicked in. I dialed 9-1-1 and then asked another bystander to request help from the mall's security. The beauty of 9-1-1 is that it is simple and actionable. What emergency training to your volunteers need? It, too, must be simple and memorable. There must be only one or two things to do in an emergency. Make them clear and memorable. Ask questions like, "Do people know where to gather if they need to evacuate the building?" and "Does everyone have the appropriate phone number of the person in authority?" Assess the legibility of maps and routes provided in various rooms. Review where the defibrillator is located. (It shouldn't be behind a locked door!) Familiarize yourself with what protocols are in place if the power goes out. The time to prepare and to train for an emergency is *before* the emergency. While an emergency is often a scary moment, training reduces the stress of the event.

Cable Cutting

"Pastor, I'm hanging by a thread!" You've probably had a conversation with someone who has said these words, or words like them. They're ready to quit—perhaps because a relationship is strained, a problem has gone unsolved, or they're just plain tired—but they're braving a conversation with you before doing so. The next time you're in that conversation, start by saying "Thank you!" As uncomfortable as these conversations can be, how else would you have known? Second, silently thank God (and probably someone else) that the thread holder had more than one thread keeping them connected. If someone's "hanging by a thread," it's because someone took the time to tie it. Training is an exercise in tying threads. Just as a cable is made up of small cords wound together, training is about winding a stronger connection to the person.

But at the same time, a time will come when everyone needs to quit a ministry. There are any number of reasons people need to quit serving in a ministry. The ministry might be radically different from what they expected (this is why "Task," the subject of the previous chapter, is so important). They might have said "Yes" too hastily. They might be entering a season of change that requires a reordering of their commitments. When people need to quit, they need to know how to quit. They need to know *how* to cut the cable. Train people how to quit well as part of initial training or else they will quit poorly later on. It's better to quit two weeks too early than two weeks too late. A burned-out, bruised, discouraged, disillusioned, disappointed volunteer can do years' worth of damage in just a couple of hours over a couple of weeks—and perhaps with the best of intentions—because they didn't know how to quit. While the specifics will differ depending on the ministry, good quitting usually involves allowing a brief time for a replacement to be found (although this might not be possible), providing an opportunity to say thank you and/or goodbye, and a chance to identify and pass on what has been learned. Allow those who are leaving to help improve future training.

There is one terrible reason that people quit: They run out of fuel. Everyone runs out of fuel at one time or another, but the best time to fill people up is not just before they hit empty. Refilling at the last moment might work once or twice—an encouraging word, a renewed vision, a promised change—but if someone hits empty again and again, they will grow cynical. Use training sessions to energize and encourage. Remind people of the valuable work they're doing. Tell them when they've done well. Work, even when it is meaningful, is draining. It takes effort. Give people opportunities to rest and recover the various resources needed to serve well. This might be physical, emotional, or spiritual. Training is about skilling up and filling up.

Train Tracks

Trains run on parallel tracks. It's not that they can simply coexist, but that one side of a train track needs another side. In training lay leaders, the following aspects always go together.

Train formally *and* informally. Formal training means that you will need to establish budgets, curriculum, spreadsheets. You will want to invest in training, know what people are learning and when, and who has gone through what training. But don't let this keep you from informal training. Lend a book and set up a coffee to talk about it. Share teaching videos with people who come to mind in the moment.

Train systematically *and* personally. Build training into the church's rhythm and calendar. Have different training levels that address different discipleship levels. Intentionally focus on head, heart, and hands at different times. Train personally by letting people accompany you as you do ministry. John was one of the most influential pastors and evangelists I ever knew. We did pastoral visitation and evangelism together when I was in college. I learned visitation by *doing* visitation. When I was training a church's lay pastoral care team to do nursing home ministry, we went to a nursing home together and debriefed the experience. Allow your personal ministry to be ministry training.

Train onsite *and* offsite. Training onsite is helpful because people need to become familiar with the ministry setting. Just like you're always a little more comfortable to act in your own home, feeling at home in the ministry setting alleviates some of the stress. But training should also be done offsite. Budget training funds to have offsite training trips. They don't have to be long. A small team visiting another church within driving distance on a Sunday morning can produce creative conversations over lunch and on the road. Philosopher Charles Taylor talks about the social imaginary that a culture inherits. Churches can develop their own ministry imaginations. Our local church and denominational traditions and experiences give us initial eyes to see, but they also put blinders on us. Being offsite can stretch and reform and refine the ministry imagination. Imagination can be especially engaged in community or teams-based learning. When teams of at least two or three people are sent for training, not only is the imagination sparked in the moment, but conversations can carry on well beyond the training.

Train with theory *and* in live settings. My dad was an educator his entire career. He was a teacher, vice principal, principal, and director. Even after he retired, he was a school board member and a teacher evaluator. He loved teaching and he loved teachers. He was invested in education. But he also knew that some training could only happen in the classroom. "Son," he once told me, "a teacher can have perfect lesson plans, but if they can't control the classroom, they're sunk." Likewise, training should involve theory and theology, but some of it needs the live setting, too. One of the best ways to keep these tracks connected is through case studies. Provide realistic but challenging scenarios based on real situations and ask, "What would you do?" Contrary to our intuition, it's okay to disagree in these settings. Why? Meetings expert Priya Parker says that part of a good gathering is causing good controversy because it helps us learn to disagree.[42] Because the toughest situations often bring up conflicting feelings in the moment, it helps to get them started ahead of time.

Conclusion

Some churches have had sporadic training. Some have had none. Churches might even be a bit suspicious of it. In these situations, the right setting will be even more important. I have been to various training sessions that were more about covering liability than anything else. Remember that ministry training is spiritual formation. And because it's spiritual formation, there should be fun and laughter. While I didn't pick up a lasting love for trains from my host, I still had a wonderful experience. I didn't lose my evening to my host's love of trains. I was lost *in the evening* because of my host's love for trains. May the same be said of ministry training in the church because of the Lord welled up within us by his Spirit.

CHAPTER 6

Track: Managing the People in Ministry

Do you not know that in a race all the runners run, but only one gets the prize? Run in such a way as to get the prize.

—1 Corinthians 9:24

KRISTA WAS RUNNING IN THE WRONG LANE. Being the most gifted runner in the race helped to make up for the running misstep, but it put her at a significant disadvantage. In an 800-meter race, runners begin at staggered points and then move toward the inside lane after the initial leg. But Krista didn't. Beginning the race in the third lane, she ran the first two laps of the 200-meter track right there. Her coach failed to get her attention;

she was so locked into her pace, posture, and breathing. He got everyone else's attention, though. "She's still leading the race, Coach!" someone called out. "But she's running so much more than everyone else," he lamented.

At least it was only a practice race and not the actual event. Krista's coach made sure she knew the rules so that she could achieve pinnacle performance in competition. But every ministry, every time of service in the local church is the actual thing. The actions and attitudes of the pastor, lay leader, minister, and volunteer matter. Every time. People are watching to see how mentors, models, moms and dads serve, especially within the family of faith. Children, teens, seekers, and saints are keen observers—all of them.

Yet ministry is also practice. Ministry is practice for the coming kingdom. It's formation. It's development. God uses service as a means of grace, a way of communicating his sanctifying and sustaining power. The classroom, church gym, outreach center, spontaneous conversation—and more!—can be a site of sanctification and healing.

I don't think I've ever spoken to a pastor whose favorite pastoral duty was management. While some managers might happen to care for the soul, pastors are required to. I know some pastors who think management is the very antithesis of their calling, but I contend that good management is essential to leadership in the church. Management matters because people are watching those deployed in lay leadership and ministry. And management matters because the lay leader is a person on the way to Christlikeness. The ebb and flow, risk and reward, ins and outs of ministry not only grow skills but souls. Holy tempers are strengthened and exercised in acts of mercy and ministry.[43]

While the context is slightly different, Paul's words to the Corinthians ring true: Leaders are at work with the people for the people's joy (2 Cor 1:24). And people's capacity for joy is connected with their Christlikeness. While you can't manage people into being joyful, management can help to provide a sanctifying context in which one's capacity for joy grows.

Paul also uses the competition of running in terms of mission (1 Cor 9). He praises the discipline of the athlete. Management, *tracking*, is about helping others to compete well in the arena of ministry so as to be fruitful for Christ and to be formed into Christ. Because management can feel formal and intimidating, I use the word "tracking" to make these key actions more personal. Tracking means intentionally attending to a person in the task they've been given, or to the wider ministry in its mission and aims, to provide resources, correction, encouragement, support, or a change to promote faithful effectiveness. Because that's a mouthful, I try to remember Krista's story. When her coach was able to make a simple correction, it made a huge difference.

So, with the image of a coach, runner, and race in mind, why do we track?

First, we track to make sure runners are effective. While Krista started in the correct lane, it soon became the wrong one. Krista was running the race, but she lacked efficiency. Some lay leaders and ministers are in the wrong lane, serving diligently but not as effectively as possible. People might be doing what they were trained to do, but their current way of doing things isn't the most fruitful.

Second, we track to see if runners have shifted lanes. While many eyes watch official races to ensure standards of fairness, ministry "runners" can end up taking on more tasks or changing roles along the way. Tracking is about knowing roles and duties amid unexpected changes. Here, the concern is not effectiveness, but proper ministry fit and necessary resources.

Third, we track to keep people in the ministry race. Recall how difficult it was to recruit someone into ministry. How hard was it to ask someone? How much casting, tasking, and training did it take for this person to be involved in ministry? That's a lot of work! Recall the hopes someone had or the spark with which they said yes. Tracking is meant to *retain* the asked, recruited, and trained. Sometimes this happens by refreshing runners. Charles Farhadian says that refreshment involves taking joy in accomplishments and satisfaction in achievements.[44] Sometimes tracking is helping someone to look back at the race that's been run so far. Unfortunately, sometimes church leaders take a cue from the satellite, internet, or cable company: They are always after the new customer. Energy is devoted to securing new volunteers. Tracking is about encouraging steady runners.

Fourth, we track to help people finish the race well. Ministry seasons come to an end. If refreshment was to keep runners in the race, tracking is done to help runners bring a race to completion, helping them to finish well rather than sputtering to a sudden stop. Tracking is *not* about begging someone to stay in the race.

Alice was an every-week volunteer. She taught her children's Sunday School class diligently and consistently. No one knew she was quitting. There were no (obvious) signs. But when she quit, she never came back. A good tracking system might have helped to keep Alice in the ministry race or to help her come to a healthier finish. It might have kept her from giving up running (ministry) altogether. Without a good tracking system, the distance from "Every week" to "Never again!" is a short step.

Fifth, we track to make sure runners are suited for the race. Krista excelled at middle distance races, but she was not a sprinter or a long-distance runner. Not all runners are suited for every race. Likewise, not all lay leaders and ministers are properly suited for every ministry opportunity. And sometimes we only find that out after the initial competition.

Sometimes runners outgrow the race. We should expect people to grow in specific skills, overall ability, and Christlike character. We should expect God to raise up more leaders. Speaking from the context of nonprofit organizations,

Leslie Crutchfield and Heather McLeod Grant write, "[Non-profit organizations] don't hoard talent; instead, they share it with the field."[45] How much more should this be true of churches! People should have a sense of belonging *in* the church but not belonging *to* the church. They belong *to* God. Churches must be intent on developing people and releasing them into ministry that benefits God's wider kingdom. If we don't track, we might leave some runners in the wrong race.

Sixth, we track to know when the race is over—even if the runners want to keep running. OK, while I don't have any real-life examples of runners who kept running a race after it was over, I have known a ministry or two (or ten) that kept on rolling long after it was effective or had any significant mission.

Seventh, we track because some runners have been injured along the way. Some runners let everyone know about an injury and others suffer in silence. Tracking helps us to see the silent sufferers, the injured runners. "The pastor's special charge is to care for the people of God by speaking and showing and by being and doing God's truth and love. Success in ministry is determined not by numbers (e.g., people, dollars) but by the increase of people's knowledge and love of God."[46] Sometimes we know God's love when the pastor takes time to attend to the runner's injuries.

Finally, we track to show someone is paying attention, that there's an invested spectator and a caring coach. It's tempting to track out of necessity, believing, "Well, if I don't track, *no one will.*" This might be true. But what's even worse is when someone else who doesn't care about the race or runners is tracking. Ministry leaders and volunteers can receive lots of compliments, or none. And they can receive critical comments, not-so-subtle suggestions, and cranky complaints. It's not only the recipients of ministry who complain. Runners can be their own worst critics. The enemy has a two-tier attack: to make people think lower of themselves and then to become bitter about this self-critique. Caring coaches track to intercept, challenge, and bandage these self-imposed wounds.

Tracking Hurdles

Management is hard work. Tracking is challenging. There's no getting around it. But we can overcome some of its hurdles.

First, we must overcome the hurdle of *unfamiliarity.* Tracking can feel *strange.* So strange, we might even ask, "Am I supposed to be doing this?" Frankly, it can feel unspiritual to talk about a volunteer's performance. But tracking is a way to communicate care. Management expert Ken Blanchard writes, "People are motivated to do things that provide them with feedback on results. Feedback is important to people. We all want to know how well we're doing. That's why it is essential for an effective performance review system to provide ongoing feedback."[47] Management is showing that we're paying attention to hard work and that it matters.

Let's look at it from another angle. Do we only want people serving and leading who never want to know how they're doing? Do we want people who don't care about their ministry effectiveness? If you were hiring an employee, would you want one who never wanted to improve?

Second, we must overcome the hurdle of *difficulty.* Tracking is not only strange work; it is hard work. Organizational theorist Russell Ackoff says, "Managers do not solve problems; they manage messes."[48] Tracking requires observation, interpretation, correction, and application—especially when ministry messes have been made. We will look at these components in more detail shortly.

Third, we must overcome the hurdle of *bad experiences*. Many of your people—perhaps you—have experienced a management nightmare. Here's Blanchard again: "When people are attacked or not dealt with truthfully, they lose respect for their organization and pride in their work."[49] As a result of management nightmares, people might be reluctant to receive any kind of tracking from the pastor that feels like management. And some pastors might be reluctant to do the work.

However, bad management can be active or passive. Bad management not only includes unnecessarily harsh reviews, unfair and unclear expectations, and selective performance observation, but also under-resourcing, laissez-faire attitudes, unattended leadership failures, and unaddressed incompetence among leaders or peers. Bad management is a guarantee if you don't do the work.

Here I find the distinction between hurt and harm to be very helpful. Hurt happens when there is any kind of pain—even if the pain is necessary. Breaking a bone to reset it hurts, but it is necessary if the arm is to function properly. On the other hand, harm happens when there is willful incompetence, haste, apathy, or evil intent. While lack of ability, lack of attention, and lack of virtue bring about pain, it is not pain with a purpose. It is harm.

Which of these hurdles is the first to overcome? Unfamiliarity? Difficulty? Bad experience? They all need to be overcome at some point. Perhaps you've already overcome one or two because of your personality, prior job experience, or effective modeling. Perhaps you still have three hurdles to leap, but don't become discouraged. No one is an expert at tracking without having done the work. The truth that all ministry is already the race but is also practice applies to management. Tracking really matters. And tracking is also practice. When we have this mindset, our tracking is already on the way to running the race well.

So now we must intentionally see tracking as ministry. We must avoid practical atheism when it comes to tracking. Observation, interpretation, correction, and application must all be kept as theological practices.[50]

Tracking Takes Observation

Krista's coach could coach her because he had observed her running technique. He watched her run. He knew her natural tendencies, bad running habits, and so on. But he also watched her race. He watched not just in practice, but in competition when the pressure was just a little higher. This kind of observation takes time and attention. But observation in the church is done not strictly for ministry tips, tricks, and cues, but as a kind of intercession. Our great High Priest, Jesus, sympathizes with us in our weakness (Heb 4:15). Moreover, John's picture of Jesus as a priest is him washing the disciples' feet (John 13:1–17). In that priestly act of cleansing, Jesus took the form of a servant. Management that is sympathetic and servant-oriented is a must in the church. It is intended to present people spiritually healthy before God even as we are aware of our own need for Christ's health. Priests were involved in many aspects of the people's lives. Likewise, what I call "priestly observation" is not simply for ministry effectiveness but for the whole of a person's life. Observation relates to the priestly work of hearing confession. Watched closely enough, a person's life is a kind of confession on display. Priests hear confession not to announce failure, but to pronounce forgiveness.

Priestly observation can take many forms. One can observe by soliciting feedback and experiences through email, texts, focus groups and team debriefs, surveys, one-on-one coffees, impromptu conversations, and more. In both written and verbal form, the critical incident technique can help to form effective questions. The critical incident technique frames questions in terms of extreme experiences—best, worst, most, least, and so on. For example:

- What was the best part of your day?
- Tell me about a time you felt least equipped.
- When are you most effective? What are you doing in those times?
- What was the worst part of that experience?

Here are seven encouragements as you plan out how you will do priestly observation. First, observation needs to be *specific*. If a person is frequently observed to be late, don't have a general sense of them "always being late." When were they late? What days? How late were they? This is not to nitpick or to cut a person a thousand times, but to develop good interpretation (the next step after observation). Facts and details are your friends.

And write down your observations. Don't rely on memory.

Second, some observation needs to be *in the field.* Be in the field by visiting small groups in people's homes, attending youth events on Friday nights, and walking around to see ministries on Sunday morning. I know this can be so time consuming and difficult. While some pastors can do walkabouts more easily because of the size of their pastoral staff, observing people in the field of ministry is important for everyone because it allows you see with your own eyes and sense with your own intuition.

Third, observation should be *noticeable.* Tracking is seeing reality, but there is more than that. Leaders must be seen to be seeing. This is not to create a false impression; it is to form a true impression that the leader cares about the ministries of the church. When people know the leader cares enough to pay attention to the ministries, then they also know the leader cares for the minister. They know their work matters; they know that *they* matter.

Fourth, observation needs to be *soon after starting and soon after quitting.* When do you start tracking? Day one of the volunteer's service. And when do you stop tracking? The day after you've talked to the person who has left the ministry. In both cases, think about these questions: What did they see that others have stopped seeing? What challenges did they experience? Did their morale and excitement wane? If you don't have any new volunteers or ministers, then act as though it's day one. Treat them as brand-new volunteers; be excited about their service and leadership. Now, sometimes I'm told, "But, Aaron, you don't want to set your people's expectations for being observed too high because you might not live up to it." My response to this is, "You want to have high expectations of your leaders and ministers, but you don't want them to have high expectations of you?"

Fifth, observation needs to be *consistent*. Schedule when you will do observation. It can happen spontaneously, but it also needs to be scheduled—perhaps quarterly but at least annually. Consistent observation means captured observation. This includes a data management system that provides appropriate information about the volunteers that are serving and about the ministries that are being overseen.

Sixth, observation discerns *needs*. But ministry needs are a bit like Pharoah's dreams: People know they have them, but they don't know what they are and they don't know what they mean. They might have common needs, but in different quantities. Here the critical incident technique is helpful. If a person expresses a wonderful experience of receiving a gift from one of their leaders, but it only happened once, then you know they appreciate gifts and that they need them more often. One of the needs we have as human beings is to have our suffering acknowledged. On a related note, we often need to acknowledge that we have seen suffering. Observation gives space for both—to acknowledge suffering and to have someone tell about the suffering they've witnessed while serving in ministry.

Seventh, observation is far more about *what someone is doing right than what they are doing wrong.* We too often think of catching people in the wrong. But what if we try to catch people doing good? Priestly observation is this kind of catching. Catch people doing right and cheer them on. When you focus more on competence than on self-esteem, you increase the likelihood of people repeating the effective behavior, which then leads to self-efficacy. People are willing to be models when they sense they are doing something worth copying. Tracking for what is right means taking note of wins along the way. When did a ministry hit an objective? When did a team achieve an aim? When you see this, say it! And when you hear about it—perhaps through conversation, testimony, or email—tell it!

Tracking Takes Interpretation

You have observed a whole lot. You have observed strengths and weaknesses. You have seen successes and struggles. You have sensed momentum and malaise. As a leader, you've captured these observations about individuals and ministries as a whole. *But what does it all mean?* That part isn't immediately clear. At least, it shouldn't be.

The story of Rehoboam illustrates just how important sagely interpretation is. It's hard to follow a hero, but that's what Rehoboam needed to do. Well, a kind of hero, anyway. While he worked the people hard, Solomon, Rehoboam's father, was also known to throw extravagant parties. He could balance out the hard work with hard play. When he died, the people were most concerned about the work. They wanted a new labor policy. If they got it, they would be loyal (1 Kgs 12:4). While some advisors told Rehoboam it was a good deal, others told him it wasn't. Younger advisors told

Rehoboam to keep a heavy hand. It was bad advice. The result was a divided nation, with some following Jeroboam, a labor leader (1 Kgs 11:28).

Interpretation is vital because humans are meaning-making beings. We assign meaning to blinking lights, bookmarks, and colored balloons. Meaning is so wrapped up in our everyday navigation of the world that we simply take meaning for granted. We conflate what we see with what it means: "What you see is what you get!" And most of the time, this works. We navigate the world at a remarkably sophisticated level just to make it through the day. However, we also get meaning wrong. We apply meaning to observation rightly—until we don't. The result of these false assumptions is so often emotional pain and leadership missteps.

What does being ten minutes late consistently actually mean? Does it mean a lack of care or does it mean overcommitment? Or does it mean the structure or timing of the ministry just don't fit the person's schedule? On the other hand, what does a person's ministry enthusiasm and frequent yes to requests mean? Does it mean commitment to the mission and thriving in loving service to God? Or does it mean a pursuit of connection outside closer relationships? Tragic as it is, ministry can become a devious distraction from spouses and children. Meaning isn't immediately clear.

Part of the reason that meaning is not always clear is because ministry has several factors. There are personal factors, systemic factors, and structural factors. Personal factors range from individual schedules to personality to individual skills—anything that is tied to an individual. Systemic factors include training processes, resourcing, ministry schedules—the rhythms and routines that make up the ministry. Finally, there are structural factors. These include flowcharts of oversight or ministry support, personnel (including number of team members and team makeup), the nature of the physical space, and overall budget considerations. It's not always easy to distinguish systemic issues from structural issues. I tend to think of systems as more day-to-day and detailed, whereas structure is more permanent but hidden from plain sight.

Sagely interpretation is vital. One way to invite wisdom is to include more than one person's observation. Sagely interpretation takes conversation—honest and candid conversation. While priestly observation focuses more on the right than on the wrong, wisdom requires an assessment of all observation. Sagely interpretation doesn't completely set aside and ignore the observer's own intuitions or hunches or tentative understandings. It just recognizes that our observations are incomplete and our meanings are not necessarily true. Be empathic. Listen to the heart of those you're leading.

Keep interpretation connected with observation. Because ministry can be a means of God's grace, it will not only build up; it will also tear down and uproot. Service can expose parts of our lives that otherwise remain hidden. Ministry and service in the church will be used by God to break idols and crucify our pseudo-selves. Be open to hearing deep meaning as the sage.

Tracking Takes Correction

Imagine Krista's coach made excellent observations of her running technique and her performance in competition and that they were able to work out what was happening and why it was happening. Perhaps Krista was running a certain way because of a nagging injury. Or perhaps she kept a wider angle on the track because she was afraid of being tripped by another runner. Or perhaps she held back in the final competition because of negative self-talk. And yet, after observing carefully and interpreting wisely, they made no changes. What would have been the point? Why go through the work of observation and interpretation to leave everything the same? I'll tell you why I have done the first two steps but ignored the third: I didn't know if people would follow my lead. I didn't know if people would take my coaching. I didn't know if they would track with me. People don't like change—whether personal or organizational. Including me. But tracking requires correction. On the other hand, we resist correcting incessantly. Even the most amicable coaches, if they correct too much, become irritating and feel overbearing.

Correction is needed in two distinct, painful situations. The first is when people have the right values but not the right performance. This can pain the coach's heart. In this situation, be careful not to bruise, crush, or discourage. The second is when people have outstanding performance but do not display important values. In this case, we do not want to berate, condemn, or condone. It can be tempting to ask, "Don't they know their attitude stinks?" or "Don't they know they need some help?" I have found that people with these kinds of shortcomings often don't know, perhaps either because they are so nice that no one has ever told them or because they are so hard-edged that no one has dared to tell them.

Prophetic correction is setting a general direction or naming an area needing attention. This does not need to be extreme. Correction can include *turning*—complete reversals of behavior. But a lot of correction involves *tuning*, making moderate or even small adjustments to things that are being done mainly right. Correction might also mean *retraining*. If basic practices or policies are not being followed, the person must be retrained in key elements of the role. Correction is also encouragement. Prophetic correction must always be hopeful, avoiding debilitating shame. As strange as it sounds, find areas that the person is doing well and affirm their competence in these areas. Let competence build confidence to correct other actions.

Prophetic correction does not avoid conflict; in fact, it is often a context for conflict. I don't think we're supposed to enjoy conflict, but trying to avoid it does not preserve harmony. Here are some encouragements to engage in conflict with conviction and compassion.

Seek the right temperature. Leadership involves not only cooling down heated situations but also heating up cool situations. Another way to think of this is that prophetic conflict accurately discerns the level of conflict. I've observed a strange dynamic in conflict. When people hate conflict, they can ramp up a relatively minor conflict to a significant level in order to engage in conflict. Without ramping up their frustration, they aren't able to act, so what is actually a three or four on the conflict scale becomes a seven or eight. Prophetic correction seeks the right temperature.

Do not force agreement. Early in my ministry, I met with a volunteer to encourage him. He was a fairly young Christian and new to church, but eager to serve. He had many gifts and I wanted him to know it. As the conversation was winding down, he brought up an area of character that others had challenged him on. He wondered what I thought. I started gently to correct him, but when he disagreed, I continued to build the case. I thought that if I could convince his head, I'd also win his heart. It didn't work. Avoid the temptation to convince people you are right. Let them disagree. Let them be disappointed.

Do not compromise on core values or convictions. Rare is the person who has not compromised in this way at some point. I've learned that if you compromise, you should resist the temptation to become bitter with others. Don't be frustrated with others because you didn't follow your convictions.

Avoid triangles. Triangles happen when someone wants to add a third person to help with the stress of a relationship. Don't engage in conflict through another person, and resist requests from others for you to become the third person.

Tracking Involves Application

Finally, correction must be applied. Without application, tracking is incomplete, and the whole process of observation, interpretation, and correction fails. Worse, it can lead to cynicism and wounding. Correction without application will often result in injury—hurt feelings, confused ministers, and hampered ministries.

Application is always situation-sensitive. It might involve resourcing people, removing people from roles, reassigning people to new situations, requiring further training, or rewarding for consistent and effective service. It might involve retiring a ministry, reassigning designated space, or resetting ministry goals. Yet four principles apply across contexts.

Be strategic. Strategy is about actions, plans, policies, and other resources brought together to achieve a significant aim. It's often helpful to bring other potential stakeholders into corrective conversations to see a strategy's potential side effects. There can be relational side effects when a key leader's relative receives correction. One ministry can be affected when another changes its programming.

Be specific. Does an attitude need to be developed? Does an action need to be increased, decreased, started, or stopped? Does a budget need to be increased? How will this be done? Think it through in steps and details and make sure that all links are known. If there are lines of leadership, make sure that everyone with a measure of authority knows the specifics. Make clear connections from the correction to the application.

There's another side to being specific. Sometimes we try to change systems to overcome personal shortcomings. We can also hope that structural changes will fix systemic breakdowns.

This can be a means of avoiding conflict. Being specific means addressing personal factors when personal factors need to be addressed, systemic factors when systemic factors need to be addressed, and structural factors when structural factors need to be addressed.

Let me give an example of avoiding conflict by changing the structure. A strong-willed and talented follower is operating outside of the rules or against policy. Perhaps they're difficult to lead. It might not be blatant, but it is noticeable and consistent, and it needs to be corrected. Ironically, it's very easy to give this follower more responsibility, hoping they will rise to the occasion. Correction by promotion is a subtle and powerful temptation. But this is often correcting personal factors with systemic or structural changes. It's deceptively easy to think, "With more responsibility, then they'll see and make the necessary changes in their character and conduct!" It's possible; they might "get it." But they might not. With a promotion, they might not just be a source of trouble to a few, but the source of discord to even more—especially if they have a leadership bent and a strong personality. Don't change systems or structures to fix personal problems.

Be speedy. When the leader finally knows correction is needed, they're already behind. Followers, peers, parents—they already know it. So, when the leader catches up, they must implement correction with speed. Refusing and unduly delaying correction leads to cynicism and skepticism.

But speed can be tricky. I do *not* mean that correction should be applied in a hurry. Speed and hurry are different things, and application should avoid hurry. Let's go back to running. The fastest runners do not run haphazardly. They run with precise technique. And the fastest runners are powerful. Application can be done with great speed, but only when there is focus and structure and power.

Urgency blurs the difference between speed and hurry. While urgency inspires hurry, urgency requires speed. This is why consistent priestly observation is vital. If you have not done good observation consistently, it is very difficult to act with speed because you might lack information or context. Even if you remain calm in the midst of urgency (which is good!), if you have not done consistent observation and interpretation you will be acting with hurry rather than with speed. It might simply be the case that you haven't had time to observe and interpret and discern correction in a timeline that best suits application. In these situations, you can't keep from acting, but be aware of its costs. Too many crises met with hurry lead to chronic anxiety in the organization.

Be supportive. Some folks only need to know the plan and they can't be stopped. They respond to strategic, specific, speedy correction. Others will need some help along the way. To help them, you will need to see how the application is working, whether it's achieving the correction, what side effects have slipped in. One of the most important ways to express support is to give permission for people and teams to fail. In *The Human Condition,* Thomas Keating writes, "The spiritual journey is not a career or a success story. It is a series of humiliations of the false self that become more and more profound."[51] Failure would be an utter disaster except that God picks us up. The best way to ensure no growth is to demand no failure.

The only way to fail well is to learn from the failure. If nothing was learned, then the failure is final. Wring every bit of knowledge out of the painful experience, letdown, or miscommunication. This might take time. Some things can only be learned when there is appropriate distance between us and the event. And once failures have yielded their insights, entrust them to God and step forward in faith. Don't dwell on them. Leaders help by developing empathy in themselves and others. Tell stories of failure and growth. Share your own insights from failures along the way. Testify to God's transforming grace personally and organizationally. Develop a profound sense of faith that God works in the toughest times of life.

Tracking in Motion

Let's put the whole process together. When necessary, I will clarify if this is for a person or for a whole ministry. Otherwise, the steps should be applicable to both. Whether you are within the first ninety days of leadership or have been on the job for years, look at the calendar and chart out a good rhythm of review and identify who or what you will be tracking. Late spring often provides a good time to look backward, and the late summer provides a good time to look forward. (You might review chapter 2: Cast to prepare for this meeting.) Give yourself enough time to complete the process.

Observation. Begin by refreshing yourself with the job description or the ministry's vision or aims or purpose. Include past performance reviews, if there are any, as necessary. (You might choose not to scan prior reviews if you are new to the role and wish to have a fresh look. However, prior reviews can provide helpful context.) Take note of any expectations or metrics or goals that were part of the task's design or training. Remember the priestly component of this work. Make sure you have spent sufficient time observing. Followers sense when you've rushed observation. Finally, gather all the observations (personal observations, surveys, emails, testimonies, etc.) that you've made or collected.

Some observations for a ministry may also include confirming up-to-date background checks, insurance needs and coverages, budgets, and demographics of those serving in the ministry. (Does a ministry that serves boys and girls or men and women have only men or only women? Does a ministry that serves across ages have only one age group in leadership?)

Next, intentionally pray through these observations to invite our Lord's wisdom and his grace.

Remember, tracking is hard spiritual work. It takes courage, conviction, warmth, and empathy.

Third, have a conversation with the individual or group of ministry leaders. Start by reviewing the job description or the ministry's vision/aims and any other expectations. There might be disagreement or expectations might have changed. Pay attention to these differences because they could inform your interpretation of what you've observed. Next, share your observations and invite other perspectives. What have you missed in your observations? What have you not seen that they want you to know? Did the expectations shift? Did the original context change? Do they see and sense something different from you? The atmosphere of these conversations is vital. Observation is not about convincing the other that you've seen everything or that only what you've seen matters. It is about making sure there's a full set of observations.

Interpretation and correction. Depending on the spirit of the conversation, you can go right into this section. If things are feeling tense or if the ministry is complex and quite a bit of time has already been taken in the conversation, then you can also take a break. This can be a few minutes or a few days.

When you return, try to achieve a common understanding of what has been observed and the general direction things need to go. At this point, you will want to do what Patrick Lencioni calls *mining for conflict*.[52] Sometimes we have shallow agreement but disagreement on a deeper level. Sagely interpretation seeks to uncover the deepest conflict. This doesn't need to be interpersonal conflict. If the observations have yielded some breakdowns, there might be conflicts between a person's skills and their responsibilities, between expectations, and between a person's ministry heartbeat and their role.

While correction can be more general, it needs to be clear. And while agreement isn't always possible, it is very important to make sure there's a common understanding of what correction has been determined by the leader. The runner needs to know which direction to go even if the plan isn't yet specific.

Application. Depending on the complexity of the necessary correction, this can be a new conversation or part of the same one. Application requires specificity. What will be done? By whom? When? What responsibilities are changing? What expectations are being clarified? Put together, the specific actions, resources, training, and supports should be effective at achieving the correction—at advancing the person or ministry in a certain direction. Write the plan down and make sure everyone responsible for it has a copy. Finally, set a follow-up time to evaluate the plan's effectiveness. I strongly encourage ending this session in prayer, asking for God's blessing to bring about good outcomes. Psalm 90:16–17 provides wonderful language and demeanor for this prayer:

> May your deeds be shown to your servants,
>   your splendor to their children.
> May the favor of the Lord our God rest on us;
>   establish the work of our hands for us—
>   yes, establish the work of our hands.

In the aftermath of this meeting, be sure to look at the plan and use it to guide your new observations. When the cycle restarts and you're doing subsequent observations, watch if the plan is being effective. Watch for good effort and the smallest advances to cheer. At the follow-up meeting, make sure to use the same plan to guide your conversation. Don't modify the plan without assessing its effectiveness. I find it especially helpful if I have handwritten notes on the actual plan. This shows everyone that the plan matters and that the aims aren't changing. If you want to meet again to assess this plan, just use a different color of pen to distinguish between stages of implementation. A follow-up meeting is very helpful because we can fall prey to instantaneous expectations. We are tempted to believe that change must be immediately visible, and if not, nothing happened. But while frustrating, it is also beautiful that good things so often happen slowly, with effort, patience, and teamwork.

Tracking Speedsters and Stumblers

Two tough situations require a few remarks: how to track those who run faster than anyone and how to track those who keep stumbling.

When King Saul was moving toward madness, he was unable to handle the rising talent of David (2 Sam 18–19). Contrary to Saul, David was able to lead because he could handle remarkable talent among his leadership. Leadership will often rise and fall by the ability to recognize talent, recruit talent, and respect talent.

Why is dealing with talented people difficult? Talented people often function according to what Daniel Goleman calls "pacesetting leadership."[53]

Pacesetting leadership is essentially saying to followers and peers, "I'm going to go fast; you keep up." While fellow pacesetters love this kind of challenge, nobody else does. Goleman found that pacesetting leadership "destroys climate." Climate, in this context, includes the follower's sense of freedom to do their own work, a sense of responsibility to the team, fairness of feedback (including rewards), clarity on mission and values, and commitment to a shared goal. In an effort to maintain climate, leaders can think they need to eliminate talent—whether by forcing them out or by forcing them into a box. Neither is wise. When talented people are forced out of a team or forced into a box, teams are left without talent and the talented are left without teams. But God created talented people, and we need to find ways to adapt our boxes to make room for them. On the other hand, leaders can coddle talented people and invest an unfair amount of time into them compared to the rest of the team. The result is jealousy.

Instead, talented people need significant measures of freedom with accountability. Henri Nouwen says, "Community is the fruit of our capacity to make the interests of others more important than our own."[54] Talented people do not need to be left alone and talented people do not need to be micromanaged. They need to be *led.* They need to be *recognized*—perhaps publicly and perhaps privately—and they need to be *reminded* that their talents, which are significant, are in service to the wider team and mission. If talent is in service to the wider mission, then there will be community. I know this is hard work. It takes relationship, humility, personal security, and more. But, frankly, it's hard to win without talent.

Another difficult part of tracking is dealing with stumblers. Of course, the process of observation, interpretation, correction, and application is supposed to help those who are stumbling. However, there comes a time when, through consistent professional or moral failure, a person needs to be removed from ministry. If this is the necessary result, then keep a few things in mind. First, the person is not simply removed and replaced, but valued and re-placed. While a new role or ministry might not be immediate, we do hope they can serve again, if under certain conditions. If a process of restoration isn't clear right away, name an interval of time such thirty days, ninety days, or six months to revisit the question. In this in-between time, the person will still need good leadership and pastoral care. If the person doing the re-placing is not a wise choice, then enlist other support to reach out.

A break from ministry can be a time of refreshment and reorientation. However, it can also be the case that when people are necessarily removed from ministry, they are accidentally removed from community. A friend of mine is a worship leader. One of his key leaders needed to be removed from ministry for a season. However, he insisted the volunteer remain part of the worship team, though not playing at public worship. It was a condition of their re-placement in the ministry. The person was part of team devotions and events and even practiced with the team as part of the application plan. The community proved essential to their restoration.

While dealing with speedsters and stumblers is challenging, it is precisely these times when leaders can earn respect. Good leadership in these times builds community with the talented and confidence with the committed.

Conclusion

Tracking takes work. It takes a lot of attention. It takes strategic thinking, ample time, emotional investment, and spiritual intercession. The process is filled with prayers, petitions, and even paperwork. But once you know that tracking takes work, you can make rest a necessity. Management is a hidden yet heavy aspect of the pastoral role that cares for the life and soul of the people. If you take tracking seriously, allow yourself a rhythm of rest and recovery. In Psalm 4, the Israelites asked, "Who will bring us prosperity?" (Ps 4:6). Today, churches can wonder the same. Who is keeping an eye on all the people and projects? Tracking is that work. It's tiring. It's vital. People are watching. Even so, may we say with David,

> In peace I will lie down and sleep,
>   for you alone, LORD, make me dwell in
>   safety. (Ps 4:8)

CHAPTER 7

Thank: Expressing Praise to God and Gratitude to His People

The first responsibility of a leader is to define reality.
The last is to say thank you.
—Max DePree

"I'M NOT INTO THOSE WORDS YET." The claim, uttered mid-munch by my neighborhood chum, caught me off-guard. Even as a youngster, I knew something was wrong. Food had been prepared and placed before him, but when his manners were prompted—well, he just wasn't into those words. My friend's mother assured mine over the phone that her son was most certainly *into those words.*

What words? The magic ones. "Please" and "thank you."

It's not just children who can forget their manners. Eric Anicich and Alice Lee found that as people acquire more power and status, they, too, become less likely to be "into those words."[55] Unfortunately but not uncommonly, higher position can lead to less appreciation. Can you think of a leader who, upon promotion, gave less credit, acknowledged fewer contributors, took more praise, and soaked up the glory?

These are humbling, haunting claims. This is so not only because not being into these words would shame someone's mother, but also because it is contrary to Scripture. Classic literature has a way of reinforcing its most important themes with its final words. Scripture is no different. We might think of Revelation, where Saint John the Divine concludes, "Amen. Come, Lord Jesus" (Rev 22:20). Or we might think of Matthew's Gospel and Jesus's final promise: "I am with you always, to the very end of the age" (Matt 28:20). The Psalter's final word is "Praise the Lord." Thirteen times—across different contexts, for different reasons, and with different tools—we are told to praise God. The Psalms, the Bible's hymnbook, leave us praising

God for his acts and greatness, with our bodies and with our breath. "Praise the Lord" (150:6b). Famous last words to serve as refrain for the famous songs.

Just as praise is our final word to God, so thank you is the leader's final word to everyone they lead. It's as simple as it is important. You can't win if you aren't grateful.

A lack of appreciation is a terrible reason to lose a volunteer. Ingratitude is completely unnecessary. Ingratitude is a sheer failure of leadership. *And it happens all the time.* If you do not say thank you, you will lose people. You will lose people too quickly. You will lose people too easily. They might leave quietly or they might leave noisily. But they will leave. The danger in this is that leaders never hear the quiet quitters and can convince themselves that the not-so-silent ones needed to go.

What do you want your final words to be? Which words do you want to remain in the memory of your people?

Blanking on Thanking

"Thank you cards are the currency of ministry." My friend David taught me that. He didn't mean that I should use thank you cards to secure help or to "buy" ministry volunteers. He meant that there is no other currency that fits the context of ministry better than "thank you." Just as we cannot earn God's grace but can only respond in praise, so pastors have not earned people's ministry. Pastors can only respond with thank you.

When too many thank you notes are left blank, the market dries up. The leader who is low with "thank yous" is high in ministry debt. Max DePree reminded leaders that all employees are, essentially, volunteers. Whether or not they earn a paycheck or a stipend, people in the church are still serving God, and they could serve God in any number of places and local churches. What keeps them around? God does. Praise God! And thank them.

While increased power or institutional authority can dry up our gratitude, three other reasons also pop up in ministry contexts. *When we stop thinking ministry is important, we stop thanking people.* In *God Tells the Man Who Cares*, A. W. Tozer said, "How frightful a thing it is for the preacher—when he becomes accustomed to his work, when his sense of wonder departs, when he gets used to the divine, when he loses his solemn fear in the presence of the High and Holy One; when, to put it bluntly, he gets a little bored with God and heavenly things." It is easy to read that warning, take it to heart, and forget that it includes ministry. Our Lord came to serve, and service in his name is carrying on the ministry of the one whose reign is seen clearly in heaven and anticipated on earth. Ministry in Jesus's name is a small display of heaven on earth. When we become bored with ministry, our gratitude decreases.

When we stop being grateful for the church, we stop thanking people. In his classic book *Life Together,* Dietrich Bonhoeffer writes, "Let those who until now have had the privilege of living a Christian life together with other Christians praise God's grace from the bottom of their hearts. Let them thank God on their knees and realize: it is grace, nothing but grace, that we are still permitted to live in the community of Christians today."[56] Of course, frustration is far easier than gratitude. Of course, frustration is understandable. Local churches, because they are contexts of discipleship and sanctification, come with hurt feelings, misunderstandings, betrayal, and shortcomings. (There are sinners among us!) The church is a grace because, while we experience these things, we also inflict them. (And we are those sinners!) Yet the church remains, by God's grace. Without gratitude for the church, we will not express our thanks to it.

When we stop praising God, we stop thanking people. Spiritual dryness comes for us all. Seasons in the desert are even a necessary part of spiritual growth and development. I am not speaking of these experiences. I am speaking of when we have stopped being disciplined in our praise. Did you know that pastors can stop attending church? They stop attending church, not in body, but in spirit. They stop attending to the Scriptures being read. They stop singing the songs. The soul no longer ascends to God during the pastoral prayer. When we stop praising God, we stop aligning our heart and mind with his. And when we are out of alignment with God, we stop thanking God's people because God's people are in his Son and the Son is always with the Father.

Friends, recover the wonder of ministry, the mystery of Christ's glorious reign expressed through humble service. Don't become bored with ministry. Yes, we can become bored with ministry policies and management tasks, but put yourself in a place to hear a testimony or two. Discipline yourself to express thanks. Gratitude is an antidote to ministry complacence.

Thanking as a Means of Grace

When we thank, we are not scrutinizing the imperfections of the one we're thanking or the shortcomings of a ministry we're acknowledging. We don't reserve thanks for perfection or excellence. This is an important distinction from tracking. Thanking is not evaluation, coaching, or adjustment. It doesn't come with a plan. Tracking requires follow-up. Thanking is an end in itself.

Saying "thank you" means there's already a debt. Thanking is a response to a gift. When we recognize that work done for God has come from God, then expressing thanks can be a means of grace—a way that God pours his own life into us. Offered in faith, it can also be the grace of God to the one being thanked. Dietrich Bonhoeffer so often captures the nitty-gritty nature of the church and its presence in the nitty-gritty of our own lives, too. He writes, "Just as Christians should not be constantly feeling the pulse of their spiritual life, so too the Christian community has not been given to us by God for us to be continually taking its temperature. The more thankfully we daily receive what is given to us, the more assuredly and consistently will community increase and grow from day to day as God pleases."[57] When we thank people for their work, ministry, and leadership in the church, we open ourselves to receive more graciously what is being given.

When we thank God's people, our praise to God is sparked. Just as turning our praise to God inspires thanksgiving for his people, so does remembering God's people inspire praise to God. Paul thanks God for the saints in Colossae. Their faith and love inspire his praise (Col 1:3–4). Remember the apostle Paul's beautiful words to the Philippians: "I thank my God every time I remember you" (Phil 1:3). When we spend time remembering—thanking—people for their work in the Lord, then we praise God. Seeing God's children at work opens our spiritual eyes to sense God at work.

We thank people to honor God's provision. The psalmist points out that God's open hands satisfy us (Ps 145:16); when God's hands are open, we are filled up (Ps 104:28). People belong to God, not the church. He graciously supplies local churches with good workers and ministers. Consider it like this: God places his people in all kinds of local churches for good things to run wild, wide, and deep. God provides his people, his beloved children, for effective service. If children you loved could volunteer under a leader who expressed sincere gratitude or under a leader who withheld it all, where would you have them serve?

Thanking creates leadership accountability. University of Alabama football coach Nick Saban said, "Every thank you comes with an I.O.U." Once I say thank you, I recognize a contribution. And if a contribution has been made, then I have the responsibility to make one myself. How delightfully subversive! When leaders are responsible to say thank you, they become accountable to the ones they've thanked.

Nothing humbles the pastor quite like learning intercessory prayer. For me, I learned how little I prayed and how little I loved. Dietrich Bonhoeffer wrote, "I can no longer condemn or hate other Christians for whom I pray, no matter how much trouble they cause me."[58] Instead, says Bonhoeffer, intercessory prayer is a purifying act. By interceding for another in prayer we do not simply *act* like Jesus. We also *become* like Jesus who is the ever-interceding Word of God. Intercessory prayer does away not only with hatred, but jealousy, apathy, and pettiness. Thanking has a similar effect. You cannot remain jealous, apathetic, or cynical toward another and genuinely thank them consistently.

May we be humbled not by our lack of thanking, but by seeing how much others have done and given. As the psalmist said, we bless God for his angels, his ministers, his works! (Ps 103:19–22).

Planning our Thanking

One of the worst mistakes leaders can make is only to thank spontaneously. If you only thank spontaneously, you will thank according to the patterns of your life and leadership. Your thanking will be limited by your schedule, emotional rhythms, and general comfort zones. Thanking—like casting, asking, tasking, training, and tracking—takes intentionality.

Of course, you should thank spontaneously, as well; let gratitude roll off the tip of the tongue. Bill O'Brien said, "The success of the intervention depends on the condition of the intervenor."[59] It is the same with gratitude and thanksgiving. The gratitude of the team depends a great deal on the attitude of its leadership.

Thank systematically. Have a thanking plan and follow it. A thanking plan along with a grateful leader helps gratitude to become part of the church's culture. Here are some ideas to build a thanking system and culture.

First, appoint a chief thanking officer. Companies have chief economic officers, chief technology officers, chief executive officers, and more. Churches can have chief thanking officers, and if you don't have one, you're it. This is a person who delights in showing appreciation and who is intent on seeing the various contributions being made by individuals and by whole ministries. We know that many ministries require a specific leader to reach their potential. Thanking itself is a ministry!

Second, budget for thanking. Thanking doesn't require money, but money does help. I am not talking about making people into paid employees. I am encouraging leaders to recognize the value that ministers provide consistently through their service to the Lord. When we allocate funds to show appreciation, we remember that volunteers are not strictly money savers. Pastors and lay leaders cast, ask, task, train, and track because that is the work of leadership. We do not do all that work just to trim the budget.

Third, systematize knowing lay leaders, ministers, and volunteers. Beyond birthdays, anniversaries, and so on, a simple survey as part of the onboarding process can inform you of every volunteer's favorite candy bar, fast food restaurant, hobby, soft drink, snack, flowers, or author. This familiarity will help you develop ideas for how to thank people personally and meaningfully.[60]

Finally, keep a record of thanks. Know when and how people have been thanked. I know this feels antithetical to thanking. Does it really count as thanking if I count it? Yes, it does. Periodically through the year, you will find on my refrigerator a checklist that tells me which child has received which medication. With four children, cold and flu season can get a little overwhelming. Is my love for my children lessened or institutionalized because I chart when and what medicine they've received? Of course not. It could even be seen as a sign of greater care. A record helps me to make sure that each child has been medicated properly. Why would keeping a record of thanks somehow render it cold and calculated? Instead, it ensures that more people are properly and personally thanked.

One of the benefits of planning our thanking is that we can avoid flattery. Thanking isn't flattery. Flattery can falsely increase confidence and decrease our willingness to engage in strategic leadership.[61] On the other hand, genuine thanking can reduce our susceptibility to flattery because it includes naming specific competencies. People become aware of genuine skills and meaningful contribution. We may grow rightly in confidence as we grow truly in competence. Good thanking, as opposed to flattery, names the specific difference being made. Have you been personally blessed by another's ministry? Include that! Does their ministry make other good activity possible? Does it aid, support, facilitate more good running wild? Tell them! Help people to see the personal differences made by their work.

Thank You Cards and Contexts

Thank you cards never go out of style, but neither is it the only tool in the shed. Write a note. Record a video message. Craft a social media post. Send a personal text message or email. Have an appreciation dinner. Open a tab at a local ice cream shop or coffee house and tell the right folks to buy themselves a treat.

Gary Chapman's *Five Love Languages* gives a helpful breakdown of thanking categories: quality time (including pastoral care in critical situations or times of crisis), acts of service, gifts (remember to budget), words of affirmation, and physical touch. In ministry, physical touch often invites complications. I do not give a hug without asking permission. They are most frequently side hugs. A handwritten note, appropriate eye contact during a sincere thank you, and a handcrafted gift also express appreciation.

Thank corporately. People serve the community and serve on behalf of the community. Let the community express thanks as a whole.

Thank personally. Express the personal difference that has been made. Has the worker encouraged you? Relieved your stress? Expanded your influence? Operationalized an idea? Elevated a ministry?

Thank an individual. Note and comment on the time an individual has committed. Note their creativity, commitment, consistency, and care. Thank long-time servers. Thank first-time servers.

Thank a whole team. Name the effect that a whole team has had on a ministry, in the church, or in the world.

Thank publicly. Let other people see thanks being given. Communicate that this is part of the church's ecosystem. Saying "Thank you" is part of this community's identity.

Thank quietly. Some people want no accolades except for yours. They don't care if anyone else sees their contributions so long as their pastor or lay leader did.

Let's close with an example of a simple thank you note. Notice that it names specific actions and their outcomes to show the person that their work *and* its effect is being seen.

> Dear Karen,
>
> Thank you for your hard work on our team. I know that you seek out and recruit people to serve alongside you on Sunday mornings. Because of your efforts, we have a very strong and committed team every Sunday serving our children. Our children are blessed every Sunday. Thank you!

Start at the End

The apostle Paul wrote, "Rejoice always, pray continually, give thanks in all circumstances; for this is God's will for you in Christ Jesus" (1 Thess 5:16–18). Give thanks even in the midst of difficult circumstances. It's not just a good reminder to look for how God has blessed in general. It's a great way to be reminded of what and who God has provided in the church.

I know ministry can be discouraging. In this book, I've talked about ministry as good things running wild in the church, wide in the world, and deep in the believer. But I also know that ministry sometimes feels like it's coming up short, slow, and shallow. If this is your current state, then I'm impressed you've made it this far through the book. But if you've made it this far, then take just one more bit of encouragement. If you're discouraged, start with thanking. Thank God for who he has provided and thank those he has provided in the church. Find someone who is showing up, sharing their faith, and serving the church. Maybe it's your spouse. Maybe you're the only one who knows about this minister or ministry. Start with thanks. Praise God for this person. Praise God for his character and provision. Praise God with your voice. You might play an instrument or play some worship music. Allow God to open your eyes and heart and mind to others serving, too.

Now that you've started at the end, you can work through this book's whole process backward. So, next, track those you've just thanked. How are they doing? What resources could they use? What are they seeing? After this, add value through training. Help people to improve. Build morale by building competence. Redesign tasks to fit the skills of the people who are there. Play to strengths. See what can change to fit the ministry context—both in the church and in the world. Finally, see what you can see. The first job of the leader is to see and define reality. Sometimes we only see reality *after* we've stopped to count our blessings. Sometimes we only see when we take time to open our hearts with gratitude. Once you have a new reality, then you can begin casting to the church. And it started with a thank you.

Conclusion

It had been a contentious meeting. We didn't see eye to eye. We knew we wouldn't see eye to eye. But we knew that talking it out was still essential to wrap up a recent uncomfortable incident. The meeting took about an hour. I confess that as we were wrapping up, I was done. I was done listening. I was done being interrupted. I was done arguing. Then I was asked a simple question: "Aaron, do you have any final words?" I was kind of taken by surprise. It was clearly a simple bit of politeness, but I saw a possibility. I didn't think I'd have this chance. In a split second, I was ready to take it. The arrow was fitted to the bow of my tongue, and I was ready to let it fly. But God. But God put the bow away. He stowed the arrow. He softened my heart. And he placed two new words in my mouth: "Thank you," I said. I can take no credit. It wasn't a ploy; it wasn't what I was expecting. "Thank you for all the good work you do in our community. It makes a difference." The words were true. They weren't flattery. But they weren't the words of choice that I had been ready to deliver just moments earlier. And out of those two simple words and brief expression of gratitude, an opportunity developed. Whereas this meeting was originally intended to close off some shared ministry, within a year I was invited back. I am sure that invitation would not have developed had God not stowed the bow.

Who needs to hear "Thank you" from you? Who has stuck around in spite of all the reasons to drop ministry? Who is continuing to show up? Whose spirit keeps burning bright? In whom is good running deep? *Tell them.* Let them know their work in the Lord and obedience to his direction is noticed. "Thank you." It's an enchanted phrase that sparks our praise to the Lord. So, let me close with these words to you, whether you are a pastor or a lay leader. Thank you for your service in your church and in our world. It is unto the Lord.

CHAPTER 8

Start: Who's Ready to Begin?

They devoted themselves to the apostles' teaching and to fellowship, to the breaking of bread and to prayer.

—Acts 2:42

THE MISSION OF THE CHURCH IS THE MISSION of the laity. When Jesus taught his disciples their defining dispositions in the Sermon on the Mount, it was authoritative teaching that extends through time. While the mission belongs to the whole church, because the laity is so widely spread abroad in the world they must cling to Jesus's words and teachings: "You are the salt of the earth" (Matt 5:13) and "You are the light of the world" (Matt

5:14). "The laity are called in a special way to make the Church present and operative in those places and circumstances where only through them can it become the salt of the earth."[62] The laity participate and lead in this mission as they worship, witness, organize, feed, fellowship, disciple new believers and the next generation, teach, study, and more. The mission is wide and is meant to go wide in the world.

But it's hardly so simple. When I first started in pastoral ministry, I oversaw our church's discipleship ministry. As a good Wesleyan, I wanted to launch a small groups ministry. But then I heard some stories. "We already had a small groups ministry," I would hear. The results were, at best, mixed. While I was determined to relaunch a small groups ministry as a vehicle for fellowship and discipleship, I learned something very valuable: If a person has a really good experience in a small group, they will tell two or three people. If they have a bad experience, they will tell ten. I don't know that that's the exact ratio, but I do know the principle holds across more than small groups: Bad news travels faster and wider than good news. I became very intentional about who would serve as a small group leader. Even though I knew that people would grow as they served, I didn't want to throw just anyone into leadership—even when there was training, support, and follow-up.

Pastors must be careful not just with small group leaders, but with all who serve and lead in the church. Pastors are given, in part, to protect the church. At the same time, pastors know that they are "not ordained by Christ to take upon themselves alone the entire salvific mission of the Church toward the world."[63] So we must take some initial risks. No person is ever completely ready for ministry. That clergy stumble and run headlong into sin as well is a reminder that we all are dependent on the Holy Spirit for faithful living and effective service.

So, how might we get started? What might we look for in people who are ready to be asked? Who is ready to serve in leadership? Beyond that, what should lay leaders consistently be doing? It is not only pastors who are asking these questions. Conscientious laypeople are asking them, too. While we covered designing roles and responsibilities earlier in chapter 4, "Task," the following are broader guidelines. John Wesley's three general rules provide basic requirements and responsibilities for all lay leaders: Do no harm; do good; attend to the ordinances of God.

First, do no harm. Of course, this is almost too obvious, but I find it helpful to apply in a few ways, like by asking a few questions. Is the person ideologically driven? Are they overtly political and supportive of a political party? Or do they support an idiosyncratic, speculative, or tangential doctrine? Of course, these issues are a matter of perspective, but harm can be done when witness to Jesus Christ is not what shines brighter than all other convictions and allegiances. Laypeople may also do harm when ministry appears to be a distraction from other elements in life. People—clergy and laity alike—can run headlong from family and relational dysfunction into serving in the church. It might seem helpful in the beginning, but it's harmful in the end. The first converts "devoted themselves to the apostles' teaching." They were postured as learners. When laypeople are postured as learners, even when they are in leadership, then they are likely to follow this rule.

Second, do good. Laypeople must believe in the work of the local church, including the local church in which they're serving. I always want to make sure people are supportive of the mission and work of their local church. This includes a support and measure of loyalty to the pastor. Of course, loyalty is not blind; support also comes in the form of accountability. When people aren't supportive of the church in general and their own local church, including the pastor, then those they're serving and leading are a natural audience for their complaints. An encouraging spirit is also essential. Ministry is tough. Ministry can be discouraging. Lay leaders must be people who can lift spirits and brighten souls. The first converts were devoted to the local church as the body of Christ. They shared their lives in common, including their food. They risked associating with others across gender and class lines. Likewise, our allegiance to Christ must result in good—sharing of goods, including time, knowledge, and other resources with others in the faith.

Third, attend to the ordinances of God. Paul's frequent admonishment not only reminds, but calls clerical and lay leaders to be above reproach as standards of model living. Consecration to God's word and prayer (1 Tim 4:5) sets aside the pastor as a good gift, tasked with teaching (1 Tim 4). When a person is found to be living against the orders and teaching of God, then this must be addressed. There might be various kinds of service for people as they grow in Christ and live lives of ongoing repentance, but as people move forward in leadership, they must be exhibiting more and more humility and seeking to follow God's ways.

Lay leaders also follow the orders of God by setting an example in attending worship and being committed to prayer. The first converts to Christ were devoted to prayer. Jesus taught us to pray in his name so that the Father would be glorified (John 14:13–14). Lay leaders pray for the pastor, the church, their friends and families, and the world.

Jesus taught his disciples to always pray and never give up (Luke 18:1). For Luke, the persistently praying widow is a picture of the church, except that the church is not a widow, but one eagerly awaiting her groom.

Paul told the church in Philippi to pray: "Do not be anxious about anything, but in every situation, by prayer and petition, with thanksgiving, present your requests to God" (Eph 4:6). Lay leaders set an example for the church to counteract worry and anxiety with prayer. To the church in Colossae, Paul encouraged devoted prayer and prayer for the mission and effectiveness of his preaching (Col 4:2–5). Lay leaders pray for the mission of the church and the preaching of the pastor and the witness of the church.

Lay leaders pray in all seasons. James taught us to pray when we are in trouble and to respond to happiness with praise (Jas 5:13). Beyond being those who pray, leaders in the church also *ask others* to pray for them. James continues: "Is anyone among you sick? Let them call the elders of the church to pray over them and anoint them with oil in the name of the Lord" (Jas 5:14).

Being devoted to godly teaching, sharing in the life of the church, and following the ways of God, especially in prayer, are wonderful indicators of a person's readiness for leadership. Are you ready to lead the laity? Are you ready to be a lay leader?

Resources

Healthy Leadership

- Carder, Kenneth L., and Laceye C. Warner. *Grace to Lead: Practicing Leadership in the Wesleyan Tradition.* Revised edition. The General Board of Higher Education and Ministry, 2016.

Carder and Warner lay out a theology of leadership from a Wesleyan perspective that is aimed at increasing both missional and institutional effectiveness and faithfulness. Faith in the person and work of Jesus Christ creates a particular kind of leader with certain values.

- DePree, Max. *Leadership Is an Art.* Currency, 2004.

This is a brief, readable, inspiring classic in the field of leadership. From a secular and business vantage point, DePree's emphasis on the importance of *the people* being led and the implicit views of persons leaders display in their leadership is a vital, prophetic challenge to pastoral and lay leaders alike, precisely because it is not an intentionally religious book.

- Nouwen, Henri. *In the Name of Jesus: Reflections on Christian Leadership. Crossroad*, 2015.

Born out of Nouwen's own experience and vocational redirection, this book reorients leaders away from various temptations, including relevance. Nouwen emphasizes the relational and corporate nature of leadership and followership by virtue of being part of the people of God.

- Sanders, J. Oswald. *Spiritual Leadership: Principles of Excellence for Every Believer.* Moody, 2017.

With many relatively brief chapters, Sanders presents resources on replacing leaders, reproducing leaders, delegation, prayer, study, improvement, and more from a rooted and devoted Christian perspective. This book is a wonderful, profound encouragement and reminder of the nature and call of Christian leadership.

- Scazzero, Peter. *The Emotionally Healthy Leader: How Transforming Your Inner Life Will Deeply Transform Your Church, Team, and the World.* Zondervan, 2015.

After coming to a place of dysfunction and weariness in his own pastoral life and ministry, Scazzero sought a new way of exercising leadership. Focusing on the inner life of the leader, Scazzero invites readers into subversive perspectives and practices, including embracing limits in order to experience freedom.

Ecclesiology, Discipleship, Ministry, Mission

- Anderson, Keith R., and Randy D. Reese. *Spiritual Mentoring: A Guide for Seeking and Giving Direction.* InterVarsity Press, 1999.

This book introduces readers to the riches of Christian spiritual writers and guides, especially as it relates to the discipleship work of the laity. Each chapter explores a unique aspect of a mentoring relationship. This book is helpful discipleship material for laypeople who want to become more invested spiritual leaders in the church.

- Carter, William J. *Each One a Minister: Using God's Gifts for Ministry.* Discipleship Resources, 2002.

Grounded in a study of the book of Ephesians (which is included in the book), this book presents numerous chapters on contexts for and kinds of lay ministry and leadership, including ministries within the church, the workplace, and the community.

- Dulles, Avery. *Models of the Church.* Image, 2002.

This classic text introduces the reader to five different models of church, each with theologies of ministry and implicit theologies of the laity. While a local church might have an explicit ecclesiology as part of its tradition, each local church might also have an implicit ecclesiology, including theology of the laity, that these categories can tease out.

- Harrington, Bobby, and Alex Absalom. *Discipleship that Fits: The Five Kinds of Relationships God Uses to Help Us Grow.* Zondervan, 2016.

Harrington and Absalom extend the categories of a previous Youth Specialties book, *The Search to*

Belong, to show how different relational "spaces" can be discipleship contexts. Relationships ranging from the most transparent to more corporate are identified, described, and leveraged for discipleship purposes and various opportunities for leadership.

- Jones, Timothy. *Finding A Spiritual Friend: How Friends and Mentors Can Make Your Faith Grow.* Upper Room, 1998.

Spiritual friendship is a wonderful opportunity for lay leadership. This book highlights a variety of experiences that can be expected in this kind of relationship, including initiating these friendships, moving on from this kind of friendship, and the value of spiritual guidance.

- McBride, Neal F. *How to Lead Small Groups: Bible Study Groups, Fellowship Groups, Support Groups, Task Groups.* NavPress, 1990.

Small groups come in a variety of forms, with beautiful opportunities and discouraging challenges. For some, leading small groups is second nature. For others, it is completely overwhelming.

McBride provides a resource that aims to help lay leaders across a variety of group opportunities to strengthen and structure their leadership of small groups.

- Okesson, Gregg. *A Public Missiology: How Local Churches Witness to a Complex World.* Baker Academic, 2020.

This book applies Lesslie Newbigin's teaching to the twenty-first century. Okesson connects the everyday life of the laity with the mission of the church without disparaging or neglecting the importance of corporate worship and personal discipleship. Mission happens across the variety of geophysical and virtual spaces that God's people traverse, taking their values, symbols, stories, testimonies, and practices with them.

- Rainer, Thom S. *I Am a Church Member: Discovering the Attitude that Makes the Difference.* B&H Publishing, 2013.

In a readable and practical book, Rainer outlines key commitments from every member of a church who would be faithful and make an impact in their local church. Rainer outlines the vital attitudes of meaningful church membership that begin with individuals and influence their relational networks, including their family.

Theology of the Laity

- Bonhoeffer, Dietrich. *Life Together*, ed. Victoria J. Barnett, trans. Daniel Bloesch. Reader's edition. Fortress Press, 2015.

What does it mean for the people of God to be centered on Christ in thought and deed rather than simply a collection of people? *Life Together* is an enduring classic that lays out the mutual influence believers may have on one another, with implications for how the church may have a collective witness in the world.

- Vatican II. Decree on the Apostolate of the Laity *Apostolicam Actuositatem*. 1965. Accesible at https://www.vatican.va/archive/hist_councils/ii_vatican_council/documents/vat-ii_decree_19651118_apostolicam-actuositatem_en.html.

and

- Vatican II. Dogmatic Constitution on the Church *Lumen Gentium*, chapter 4. 1964. Accessible at http://www.vatican.va/archive/hist_council/ii_vatican_council/documents/vat-ii_const_19641121_lumen-gentium_en.html.

Emerging from the Second Vatican Council, these documents affirm and amplify the role of the laity in the church's mission from a Catholic perspective. Laypeople are affirmed to share in the offices of Christ, including being nourished in these offices by the sacraments.

- Kraemer, Hendrick. *A Theology of the Laity*. Westminster Press, 1958.

A vital theological and historical text on the question of the laity, this book highlights the spirit of Kraemer's own day but also orients the reader to Kraemer's ongoing role in missional theology today. Removed by a couple of generations, readers will also note critiques for contemporary missional movements that have been more pragmatically than theologically grounded in the work and person of Jesus Christ.

Notes

The prayer beginning "Almighty and everlasting God" on pages xxiii–xxiv is a fifth-century prayer for Good Friday. The sixteenth-century English reformer Thomas Cranmer presented it as one of three prayers of the day for Good Friday in the 1549 Book of Common Prayer.

1. C. S. Lewis, *Mere Christianity* (HarperCollins, 1997), 33–34.
2. G. K. Chesterton, *Orthodoxy* (Regent College Publishing, 2004), 111.
3. See A. W. Tozer, *God Tells the Man Who Cares* (Moody, 2006).
4. Karl Barth, *Church Dogmatics* III.4 (Hendrickson, 2010), 489.
5. Hendrick Kraemer, *A Theology of the Laity* (Westminster, 1958), 94.
6. Martin Luther, " Open Letter to the Christian Nobility of the German Nation Concerning the Reform of the Christian Estate," accessed February 27, 2022, https://web.stanford.edu/~jsabol/certainty/readings/Luther-ChristianNobility.pdf.
7. Robert Barron, "What Are the Laity Supposed to Be?," *Word on Fire*, December 30, 2021, https://www.wordonfire.org/

videos/bishop-barrons-commentaries/what-are-the-laity-supposed-to-be-2.

8. Charles E. Farhadian, *Christianity: A Brief Introduction* (Baker Academic, 2020).
9. Barth, *Church Dogmatics* III.4, 557.
10. Barth, *Church Dogmatics* III.4, 560.
11. Robert Barron, *Daily Gospel Reflection*, January 26, 2022.
12. Max DePree, *Leadership Is an Art* (Currency, 2004), 11.
13. Augustine, *The Confessions*, trans. Maria Boulding (New City Press, 2002), 124.
14. I owe the genesis of this thought to my good friend Dr. Lenny Luchetti.
15. C. S. Lewis, *The Magician's Nephew* (Collins, 1955), 116.
16. C. S. Lewis, "Is Theology Poetry?," *The Weight of Glory* (HarperOne, 2001), 140.
17. Hendrick Kraemer, *A Theology of the Laity* (Westminster, 1958), chapter 5.
18. Ken Blanchard, "Catch People Doing Something Right," April 12, 2017, https://www.kenblanchardbooks.com/catch-people-doing-something-right-2.
19. This idea was initially heard at the Global Leadership Summit in 2017. For the same point, but with different language, see Andy Stanley, "The 'Wow' and the 'How,'" December

18, 2017, https://globalleadership.org/videos/leading-organizations/the-wow-and-the-how.

20. Barth, *Church Dogmatics* III.4, 490.
21. For the ethics of persuasion, see Robert B. Cialdini, *Pre-Suasion: A Revolutionary Way to Influence and Persuade* (Simon & Schuster, 2016) 209–23. See also "The Science of Persuasion," *Scientific American* 284.2 (2001): 76–81.
22. Henri J. M. Nouwen, *A Spirituality of Fundraising* (Upper Room, 2011), 21–22. While Nouwen is speaking about fundraising in particular, it is a kind of asking. This insight certainly applies to more than asking for money, but also for time, commitment, responsibility, and so on.
23. John L. Drury, "6:15 - Dr. John Drury - The Call - Wesley Seminary," Wesley Seminary, accessed March 22, 2022, https://www.youtube.com/watch?v=10GdHoUMQSk.
24. Kenneth L. Carder and Laceye C. Warner, Grace to *Lead: Practicing Leadership in the Wesleyan Tradition*, rev. ed. (The General Board of Higher Education and Ministry, 2016), xix.
25. William H. Willimon, *Pastor: The Theology and Practice of Ordained Ministry* (Abingdon Press, 2002), 13.
26. Scot McKnight, *Open to the Spirit: God in Us, God with Us, God Transforming Us* (WaterBrook, 2018), 117.
27. Nouwen, *Spirituality of Fundraising*, 20.

28. Nouwen, *Spirituality of Fundraising*, 19.
29. Nouwen, *Spirituality of Fundraising*, 21.
30. Nouwen, *Spirituality of Fundraising*, 21.
31. See Aaron Perry, "#159 Dr. Beth Seversen: Why Young Adults are Leaving the Church," *Wesley Seminary Podcast*, November 19, 2020, https://podcasts.apple.com/us/podcast/159-dr-beth-seversen-why-young-adults-are-leaving-the-church/id1286343947?i=1000499397471.
32. Seth Godin, "The Cake Mix Insight," *Seth's Blog*, March 23, 2022, https://seths.blog/2022/03/the-cake-mix-insight.
33. The following is based heavily on Doug Paul, *Ready or Not: Kingdom Innovation for a Brave New World* (100 Movements Publishing, 2020), with modifications from Ori Brafman, Lance Ford, and Rob Wegner, *The Starfish and the Spirit* (Zondervan, 2021).
34. See Scott Burson, *All About the Bass: Searching for Treble in the Midst of a Pounding Culture War* (Cascade, 2021).
35. I first experienced the first two ideas with my friend and ministry consultant Dr. Amanda Drury.
36. For a wonderful introduction to systems thinking, see Donnella Meadows, *Thinking in Systems: A Primer* (Chelsea Green Publishing, 2008).

37. Dr. David Gyertson's kenotic leadership model also uses the inputs of hands, head, heart, and habits.
38. Ken Blanchard, *The Heart of a Leader: Insights on the Art of Influence* (David C. Cook, 1999) 7.
39. C. S. Lewis, *Mere Christianity* (HarperCollins, 1997), 147.
40. Ron Carucci, "To Retain New Hires, Spend More Time Onboarding Them," *Harvard Business Review*, December 3, 2018, https://hbr.org/2018/12/to-retain-new-hires-spend-more-time-onboarding-them.
41. https://churchplants.com/how-tos/6307-andy-stanley-how-to-give-em-permission-not-to-believe.html.
42. Priya Parker, *The Art of Gathering: How We Meet and Why It Matters* (Penguin, 2020), chapter 7.
43. John Wesley, "On Zeal," in *John Wesley's Sermons: An Anthology*, ed. Albert C. Outler and Richard P. Heitzenrater (Abingdon Press, 1991), 468.
44. Charles E. Farhadian, *Christianity: A Brief Introduction* (Baker Publishing Group, 2020), 117.
45. Leslie R. Crutchfield and Heather McLeod Grant, *Forces for Good: The Six Practices of High-Impact Nonprofits* (John Wiley & Sons, 2012), 137.
46. Kevin Vanhoozer and Owen Strachan, *The Pastor as Public Theologian* (Baker Academic, 2015), 22.

47. Ken Blanchard, *The Heart of the Leader: Insights on the Art of Influence* (David C. Cook, 2010), 15.
48. Russell L. Ackoff, "The Future of Operational Research Is Past," *Journal of the Operational Research Society* 30.2 (1979): 100.
49. Blanchard, Heart of the Leader, 15.
50. The following four steps rely upon Richard Osmer, *Practical Theology: An Introduction* (Eerdmans, 2008).
51. Ruth Haley Barton, *Life Together in Christ: Experiencing Transformation in Community* (InterVarsity Press, 2014), 106.
52. Patrick M. Lencioni, *The Advantage: Why Organizational Health Trumps Everything Else in Business* (John Wiley & Sons, 2012), 45–46.
53. Daniel Goleman, "Leadership that Gets Results," *Harvard Business Review*, March–April 2000, https://hbr.org/2000/03/leadership-that-gets-results.
54. Nouwen, *Spirituality of Fundraising*, 47.
55. Eric M. Anicich and Alice J. Lee, "Research: More Powerful People Express Less Gratitude," *Harvard Business Review*, April 25, 2022, https://hbr.org/2022/04/research-more-powerful-people-express-less-gratitude.
56. Dietrich Bonhoeffer, *Life Together*, ed. Victoria J. Barnett, trans. Daniel W. Bloesch (Fortress Press, 2015), 4.
57. Bonhoeffer, *Life Together*, 13.

58. Bonhoeffer, *Life Together*, 64.
59. Otto Schärmer, "Collective Mindfulness: The Leader's New Work," *Huffpost*, February 5, 2014, https://www.huffpost.com/entry/collective-mindfulness-th_b_4732429.
60. See Tyler Arnold, *Pastoral Visitation for the Care of Souls* (Lexham Press, 2022), especially pp. 75–76, for excellent, practical teaching on using such files for pastoral care and visitation. Arnold includes information that delves more deeply into pastoral support that can be wedded to these comments on thanking.
61. S. H. Park, J. D. Westphal, and I. Stern, "Set Up for a Fall: The Insidious Effects of Flattery and Opinion Conformity toward Corporate Leaders," *Administrative Science Quarterly* 56.2 (2011): 257–302.
62. Dogmatic Constitution on the Church *Lumen Gentium* (1964), 4.33, accessed July 8, 2023, https://www.vatican.va/archive/hist_councils/ii_vatican_council/documents/vat-ii_const_19641121_lumen-gentium_en.html.
63. *Lumen Gentium*, 4.30.

Works Cited

Ackoff, Russell L. "The Future of Operational Research Is Past." *Journal of the Operational Research Society* 30:2 (1979): 93–104.

Anicich, Eric M., and Alice J. Lee. "Research: More Powerful People Express Less Gratitude." *Harvard Business Review*, April 25, 2022. https://hbr.org/2022/04/research-more-powerful-people-express-less-gratitude.

Augustine. *The Confessions*. Translated by Maria Boulding. New City Press, 2002.

Barron, Robert. "What Are the Laity Supposed to Be?" *Word on Fire*, December 30, 2021. https://www.wordonfire.org/videos/bishop-barrons-commentaries/what-are-the-laity-supposed-to-be-2.

———. "Daily Gospel Reflection," January 26, 2022.

Barth, Karl. *Church Dogmatics* III.4. Edited by Thomas F. Torrance and Geoffrey W. Bromiley. Hendrickson, 2010.

Blanchard, Ken. "Catch People Doing Something Right." *KenBlanchardBooks.com*, April 12, 2017. https://www.kenblanchardbooks.com/catch-people-doing-something-right-2.

———. *The Heart of the Leader: Insights on the Art of Influence*. David C. Cook, 2010.

Brafman, Ori, Lance Ford, and Rob Wegner. *The Starfish and the Spirit*. Zondervan, 2021.

Burson, Scott. *All About the Bass: Searching for Treble in the Midst of a Pounding Culture War*. Cascade, 2021.

Carder, Kenneth L., and Laceye C. Warner. *Grace to Lead: Practicing Leadership in the Wesleyan Tradition*. Revised edition. The General Board of Higher Education and Ministry, 2016.

Carucci, Ron. "To Retain New Hires, Spend More Time Onboarding Them." *Harvard Business Review*, December 3, 2018. https://hbr.org/2018/12/to-retain-new-hires-spend-more-time-onboarding-them.

Cialdini, Robert B. "The Science of Persuasion." *Scientific American* 284.2 (2001): 76–81.

Chesterton, G. K. *Orthodoxy*. Regent College Publishing, 2004.

Crutchfield, Leslie R., and Heather McLeod Grant. *Forces for Good: The Six Practices of High-Impact Nonprofits*. John Wiley & Sons, 2012.

DePree, Max. *Leadership Is an Art*. Currency, 2004.

Drury, John L. "6:15 - Dr. John Drury - The Call - Wesley Seminary." Wesley Seminary, accessed

March 22, 2022. https://www.youtube.com/watch?v=10GdHoUMQSk.

Farhadian, Charles E. Christianity: *A Brief Introduction.* Baker Academic, 2020.

Godin, Seth. "The Cake Mix Insight." *Seth's Blog,* March 23, 2022. https://seths.blog/2022/03/the-cake-mix-insight.

Goleman, Daniel. "Leadership that Gets Results." *Harvard Business Review,* March–April 2000. https://hbr.org/2000/03/leadership-that-gets-results.

Kraemer, Hendrick. *A Theology of the Laity.* Westminster, 1958.

Keating, Thomas. *The Human Condition: Contemplation and Transformation.* Paulist Press, 1999.

Lencioni, Patrick M. *The Advantage: Why Organizational Health Trumps Everything Else in Business.* John Wiley & Sons, 2012.

Lewis, C. S. *The Magician's Nephew.* Collins, 1955.

———. *Mere Christianity.* HarperCollins, 1997.

———. "Is Theology Poetry?" Pages 116–40 in *The Weight of Glory.* HarperOne, 2001.

Luther, Martin. "Open Letter to the Christian Nobility of the German Nation Concerning the Reform of the Christian Estate." https://

web.stanford.edu/~jsabol/certainty/readings/Luther-ChristianNobility.pdf. Adapted from the translation of C. M. Jacobs. *Works of Luther.* A. J. Holman Company, 1915. http://www.iclnet.org/pub/resources/text/wittenberg/luther/web/nblty-03.html.

McKnight, Scot. *Open to the Spirit: God in Us, God with Us, God Transforming Us.* WaterBrook, 2018.

Meadows, Donnella. *Thinking in Systems: A Primer.* Chelsea Green Publishing, 2008.

Nouwen, Henri. *A Spirituality of Fundraising.* Upper Room, 2011.

Park, S. H., J. D. Westphal, and I. Stern. "Set Up for a Fall: The Insidious Effects of Flattery and Opinion Conformity toward Corporate Leaders." *Administrative Science Quarterly* 56.2 (2011): 257–302.

Parker, Priya. *The Art of Gathering: How We Meet and Why It Matters.* Penguin, 2020.

Paul, Doug. *Ready or Not: Kingdom Innovation for a Brave New World.* 100 Movements Publishing, 2020.

Perry, Aaron. "#159 Dr. Beth Seversen: Why Young Adults Are Leaving the Church." *Wesley Seminary Podcast*, November 19, 2020. https://

podcasts.apple.com/us/podcast/159-dr-beth-seversen-why-young-adults-are-leaving-the-church/id1286343947?i=1000499397471.

Schärmer, Otto. "Collective Mindfulness: The Leader's New Work." *Huffpost,* February 5, 2014. https://www.huffpost.com/entry/collective-mindfulness-th_b_4732429.

Stanley, Andy. "The 'Wow' and the 'How.'" *Global Leadership Network,* December 18, 2017. https://globalleadership.org/videos/leading-organizations/the-wow-and-the-how.

Tozer, A. W. *God Tells the Man Who Cares.* Moody, 2006.

Vanhoozer, Kevin, and Owen Strachan. *The Pastor as Public Theologian.* Baker Academic, 2015.

Vatican II. Dogmatic Constitution on the Church *Lumen Gentium.* 1964. https://www.vatican.va/archive/hist_councils/ii_vatican_council/documents/vat-ii_const_19641121_lumen-gentium_en.html.

Wesley, John. "On Zeal." In *John Wesley's Sermons: An Anthology.* Edited by Albert C. Outler and Richard P. Heitzenrater. Abingdon Press, 1991.

Willimon, Will. *Pastor: The Theology and Practice of Ordained Ministry.* Abingdon, 2002.